To

Dev[...]

dear friend + fellow

seminarian!

Wayne Ward

February, 1979

The Word Comes Alive

The Word
Comes Alive

Wayne E. Ward

BROADMAN PRESS
Nashville, Tennessee

Dewey Decimal classification: 248.5
Library of Congress catalog card number: 69-14370
Printed in the United States of America
7.5F68KSP

This book is gratefully dedicated

to
Mary Ann

through whose life the Word has
come alive for me

Contents

Introduction
The Living Word

The Word became flesh! This is the central truth of the Bible. It is the very heart of the Christian revelation. Of course, its primary reference is to the incarnation of Jesus Christ, the Son of God. God did not simply speak a word—he came as a living human being. In flesh and blood he wrought out upon this earth, in actual events, the meaning of his love and grace.

But this is the meaning of the Old Testament as well as the New! God has always been speaking through events. God's Word is always a happening! The very term used for "word" in the Old Testament (*dabar*) means "event" or "thing" before it designates a vocal sound, or writing on clay or on paper. God's Word is alive, and it gives life to everything it touches. It creates, judges, redeems, and even brings life from the grave. God's Word brought the worlds into being and sustains them at every moment. The on-going miracle of the natural order is God's Word *working!*

Embalming the Word

With such a living and dynamic reality as the vibrant Word of God, it is a tragedy thrice compounded that Bible teachers and preachers have been able to turn the Holy Scriptures into such a dead and lifeless book. How many "tedious and taste-less hours" have been spent by faithful church members in monotonous attendance upon the embalming of the Word! Thanks be unto God, the Word will sometimes jump up from the embalming table and run forth in spite of everything the intent mortician can do. But there ought to be a law against the lifeless way in which the Scriptures are handled by this army of scriptural undertakers.

The Bible is not just an archive of ancient sayings and tedious historical references. It is a living book. It speaks to us today. If we open its pages in the power of the Holy Spirit, we enter with dynamic involvement into the thrilling events through which God encountered men in history. And —even more—the Word of God will stab right through into our lives today. Across the centuries and the cultural barriers, God will bring his Word alive in our situation, in our times, in our city streets, and in our homes. This is the miracle of the living Word. God is alive. God's Word is his very life—going forth into the world to bring order out of chaos, to give light to the darkened and life to the dead.

Liberating the Word

Let the Word live! If a Bible teacher does not so handle the Word of truth that men are thrilled, judged, renewed, challenged, and blessed—he is failing in his calling. Even a simple reading of the Scriptures, without any comment whatsoever, has been known to challenge, convict, and re-create a sinful soul. It is all but incredible that well-intentioned Bible inter-preters have been able to bury this vibrant Word under such an avalanche of dogmas, commentary, and tired clichés that many young people today think the Bible is just a collection of pious, irrelevant religious meditations. Actually, it is the most exciting thing going.

The most creative, *avant-garde* youth of today has never had a thought that can match the Bible for its devastating judgment upon the status quo, its penetrating insight into a positive solution, and its guidelines for action. The living Word of God strikes this confused age with such force that it shatters the tired prejudices of men. Yet, countless people, in their smug ignorance of its truth and power, dismiss the Bible as no longer relevant. Our Bible teachers and preachers must carry a heavy part of the blame for this outrageous estimate of the Scriptures. If the Scriptures are dead and lifeless, it is because they have become so in our hands.

This present book is a call. Those who love the living God, those whose lives have been touched by his living Word, must turn again to the sacred pages. They must allow the Holy Spirit, who moved in holy men of old, to move in them—and through them to the whole world!

A Different Kind of Word

This world is filled with words. They pour out of every conceivable outlet. They pound our ears like triphammers in the high-pressure commercial. They rattle on our helpless heads in a thousand pitches, timbers, and subjects.

Yet, there is a dreadful sameness to them all. The petty circle of man's selfish little world is the prison realm from which they never escape. All our talk is about self—what the self wants, feels, hates, and plans. The world is quite literally dying for an authentic word from Beyond! Only one book in all the history of man has brought overwhelming validation of its claim to be that Word from the Eternal. Even among religious books the Bible is absolutely unique, and Christians of all ages have found it to be the inspired Word of God.

They have flocked to this fountain for spiritual strength and renewal.

In this sophisticated age, people still hunger for plain and simple Bible study. For more than twenty years this writer has seen people of differing educational levels, races, and cultures come with yearning hearts and give earnest attention to serious study of the Scriptures. No subject is more enthralling, and none makes a wider appeal—to youth or age, to the wise or simple. The pastor who will pay the price of intensive study and exposition of the Scripture and present it effectively will always have a congregation waiting upon his message. The Bible teacher who will earnestly seek to discover the meaning of the scriptural text and then apply it to the lives of the class members will always have a responsive class.

The reason for this can be simply stated: into a weary world of human sin and failure, into a sea of problems and heartache, into a life that is threatened with meaninglessness, the Word of God comes with stabbing suddenness and thrilling power! It judges and condemns our petty lives. It holds up to our homes and hearts the mirror of truth and searches out the deepest values of our lives. It turns us from self to the grace of God which liberates us from the vicious circle of lust for pleasure, power, and the possession of material things.

Because the Bible is an ancient book, written in strange languages, and reflecting an alien culture, it requires the most exhaustive study to unfold the depth of its message. It records the stormy history of a people whose works and ways are often unknown to us, and the truth revealed in the events of that history may elude the superficial reader. Yet, in style and vocabulary it is often so simple that a child can find rich treasures of meaning, while the most dedicated scholar can

how to book

never plumb the depths of its truth.

This guide to Bible interpretation is written for one purpose—to show preachers, Bible teachers, or any serious Bible reader how to discover the message of the Bible in greater depth and how to communicate it to others more effectively. This is a "how to do it" book. It is based upon many years of study and teaching of biblical theology, history, and language. It takes into account the older biblical hermeneutics (the science of interpretation), and it is also keenly aware of the so-called "new hermeneutic" which is very much in vogue in Europe. However, it attempts to break new ground and develop a distinctive approach.

The methods employed here have been discovered, developed, and applied in seminary classrooms, pastors' conferences, country churches, university lecture halls, and living-room study groups. Each method is authentically grounded in the very nature of the biblical literature itself. The methods applied to different types of biblical literature are determined by the conditions which gave rise to that particular kind of literature in the first place. The Bible is its own best interpreter, and the primary task of the Bible teacher is to clear away any obstacles so that the Bible may speak for itself.

No parochial claim is placed upon these methods. They have all been influenced and shaped by many different interpreters, and where this influence is direct or conscious it is gratefully acknowledged. All are invited to employ, adapt, or reject any of these methods as each individual reader may see fit. They are intended to help *anyone* who is trying to open up the message of the Bible and apply it to life today. If any help is given on that all-important task, the purpose of the book will be achieved.

Each chapter will be divided into two major parts: the first part will describe and explain the particular method of interpretation, and the second part will be an unadorned and direct illustration of the method. Because there will be no commentary in the course of the illustration, it will be necessary to include a brief closing section in which particular aspects of the method are cited and explained in the light of the illustration.

The particular passages which are chosen to illustrate the various methods of interpretation have been tried and proven in almost every kind of teaching situation. The analysis of each method is intended to give further guidance in the application of the same method to other passages of Scripture. It is the hope of this writer that they may open up new and rich experiences in the interpretation of the Word of God.

1

"You Are There"

I. Method

The Bible is primarily a book of events. The central event is the life, death, and resurrection of Jesus. However, the entire Old Testament is set in the framework of the historical events of the people of Israel. In the period following the Gospels, the framework of the New Testament writings is the ongoing life of the church. Even the Epistles and the Apocalypse have to be interpreted within the context of particular historical events in the early Christian community.

In this respect, as in many others, the Bible is different from all other religious books. Most religious books are composed almost entirely of meditations, mystical reflections, instructions for cultic rituals, moral concepts, or codes of law. All of these can be found, to a limited extent, in the Bible. But even where there is a law code or a description of a religious ritual, it is rooted in a particular historical event in which God revealed his truth to his people. Biblical revelation is always rooted in actual historical events, and when theological statements are taken from the Bible and torn loose from their historical moorings, they can become very dangerous.

If God spoke in actual historical events, the only way we

can hear again what God said to his people is to recover in the deepest possible way the vital reality of those events. If God had communicated his truth simply by a series of theological statements and dropped them straight from heaven, we could compile them systematically in a textbook and study them in a purely rational and logical way. Some try to treat the Bible in this way, collecting a series of theological propositions which are often terribly distorted by abstracting them from their historical setting and even interpreting them in a rational system of philosophy which is foreign to the Bible.

God revealed himself in actual events of history exactly because there is no other way to communicate personality. Revelation is not some theological statement about God— revelation is God disclosing himself personally to us. The content of God's Being cannot be expressed in words. For that matter, no person can be known simply by words. It is necessary to meet the person in actual life situations, and through the interaction of life with life some understanding can develop.

Re-creating the Situation

All events have an element of uniqueness. They are unrepeatable. There may be other incidents like them in some ways, but there can never be an event exactly like another. Time marches on, and all the powers of heaven cannot call it back and do it over again.

If biblical truth is so often couched in the language of a story, in the account of an event in history, then it is necessary to re-create that situation with such clarity and power that it lives again in our imagination. Many of the biblical stories were told around the campfire among a group of shepherds, or repeated by a father to his children as they gathered after the evening meal at the close of the day.

The truth of their experiences with God had not been reduced to certain rational theological statements, as happened later; rather, they gave their testimony of what God did in their own lives, and they left it to each hearer to respond in the way that the experience spoke to him. Events communicate a kind of truth that abstract language never can. Accounts of personal experiences speak to all ages, all cultural backgrounds, and all educational levels in a way that no other form of expression can.

Because the unique truth of God's nature and his dealing with mankind are bound up in the events of biblical history, they can be disclosed only when the contemporary reader enters into the historical event with such sympathetic understanding that God begins to speak to him through that event as he did in the long ago. In order for this to happen, one must know the history, the customs, the nuances of language and context in the biblical narratives.

The re-creation of a biblical event requires specific information from the historian and archaeologist, but it requires something more—the gift of sympathetic insight and intuitive feeling in order to enter into the experiences of another. Some of the greatest Bible preachers and teachers have been simple and uneducated people who had this rare ability to soar on the wings of holy empathy and lift a whole congregation with them. The striking element which they all have in common is this—they had the ability to make you feel that *you were there*—that these events were not simply happening to Abraham, or Jacob, or Paul, but to *you*.

When the centuries drop away and the pulse quickens with the pace of the action, when the keen excitement of the story has gripped the imagination, and when—suddenly—like Zacchaeus of old you find yourself in the center of the stage, the Word of God is just about to come alive for you. This ought to happen in every great Bible sermon or Scripture lesson, but it depends upon the skilful preparation of the interpreter and the powerful presence of the Holy Spirit. Only the One who breathed upon the Scripture writers of old can breathe upon these words and bring them alive for us today!

The Role of Historical Study

Because events take place at a point in history, it is absolutely essential that one recover the historical setting if he is to understand any event. Some people seem to despise history, but such a person is going to have a difficult time with the Bible. It is a book of history. In this it differs from most other religious books. Christianity is a historical religion. All of its claims stand or fall with certain historical events—the birth and life of Jesus Christ, his death and resurrection. To re-create the biblical events with clarity and power it is necessary to study the history, the culture, and the circumstances until one can actually become a kind of "contemporary" with the biblical people. The interpreter needs to know how they lived, how they talked, how they dressed, how they worked, and how they felt about the deepest things of life.

Because of the fantastic advances of archaeology and historical study, it is possible for us to re-create the times of Abraham, or Jesus, or Paul, with a precision which would not have been possible for previous generations. Faithful scholars have unearthed the culture, the language, the customs, and the simplest artifacts of daily life. Events which were hazy have become very clear in the light of these historical discoveries. Against the background of the Dead Sea Scrolls, the life and message of Jesus can be seen with greater clarity as the prophetic call to prepare for the inbreaking reign of God in the midst of this sinful world.

Steps to Take

Step 1. The first step to take in re-creating the biblical events is to read the biblical text until every detail of the narrative is fixed in the mind. The biblical stories were preserved orally, in some cases for hundreds of years, before they were written down. No word or detail is there just for "filling." Each detail adds something, and if it is omitted, some part of the action or the atmosphere of the narrative will suffer. Absolutely nothing can take the place of a careful and observant mastery of every detail of the biblical account.

Step 2. The next step involves the historical study of the passage. This may require a good Bible dictionary, such as the *Interpreter's Dictionary of the Bible* (New York: Abingdon Press, 1962, 4 vols.), or some other good Bible dictionary, commentary, or atlas. This is where the technical study of professional scholars is most important. Practically all seminaries and theological schools major on historical research in the area of biblical studies.

Any commentary or biblical history which will throw light upon the passage should be carefully studied. The abundant discoveries of the archaeologist have been put into popular form in dozens of publications:

Our Living Bible, by Michael Avi-Yonah and Emil G. Kraeling (New York: McGraw-Hill, 1962) and *Illustrated Family Encyclopedia of the Living Bible,* edited by Charles Kraft, and others (Chicago: San Francisco Productions, 1967) are examples.

The purpose of this step in preparation is to give the interpreter such a "feel" for the words and circumstances of the narrative that he can actually empathize his way right into the middle of the action.

Step 3. In a step that is pure drama, the interpreter must try to forget that he is a teacher ticking off points before the class, or a preacher getting off a pulpit oration, and become a creator of a historical stage upon which a divine drama is about to take place. He must literally conduct his hearers with few words in a matter of minutes into an experience which has come alive for him only after days and hours of toil and searching. This is the critical moment, and it goes without saying that the interpreter cannot conduct his hearers into an event which he has not experienced himself. If the event has not gripped the interpreter, if he cannot see it in his mind's eye, if he has not felt the quickening of the heart as he is caught up in the action, he is beaten before he starts.

Step 4. The next step is sheer grace. Only God who revealed himself through these biblical events in the long ago can speak through them to the hearts and minds of men today. No interpreter can coerce this, because God is sovereign and moves where he will. But God has promised to bless his Word, and a faithful presentation of the biblical message in all of its historical power opens up a channel through which God can strike like lightning into the stubborn and calloused hearts of men. Few thrills can match the awesome joy with which the faithful interpreter of the Scriptures sees the light break and the very presence of God reach through the biblical Word that has come alive for the hearer. Every Bible teacher knows this wondrous miracle and trembles in the humble acknowledgement that he could not bring this about himself.

Although this divine disclosure is strictly in the hands of God, the faithful interpreter will prepare for it—pray for it—and confidently expect it! God will speak through the Scriptures; he brings the Word alive.

II. Example: "Behold the Lamb of God!"

We read in Genesis 22, beginning at verse 1: "After these things God tested Abraham, and said to him, 'Abraham!' And he said, 'Here am I.' "

The older versions say that God "tempted" Abraham, but the word really means to "try" or "put to the test." And God said, "Take now thy son, thine only son Isaac, whom thou lovest, and get thee into the land of Moriah; and offer him there for a burnt offering upon one of the mountains which I will tell thee of."

How could God ask such a thing? How could Abraham be sure that God was really asking him to offer up his beloved son of promise on the altar of burnt offering? After all, the very life of little Isaac was a miracle, fulfilling God's promise. Long ago, in the distant homeland of Abraham in Chaldea, this same voice had called him into the grand adventure—into a land that he had never seen, for a purpose that was glorious:

"Get thee out of thy country, and from thy kindred, and from thy father's house, unto a land that I will show thee: and I will make of thee a great nation, and I will bless thee, and make thy name great; and thou shalt be a blessing . . . and in thee shall all the families of the earth be blessed" (Gen. 12:1-3, KJV).

Through this son of promise a nation would come—and through this nation the divine Deliverer would come—bringing the blessings of salvation to the nations of the world.

Abraham had not hesitated in his response to that call. Gathering his family and possessions, he had journeyed across the trackless deserts, down through the beautiful valley between the Lebanons under snow-capped Mount Hermon, and into the strange new land of Canaan. Even there, in the land of promise, famine struck! Hostile tribesmen joined forces to harass and destroy him—but through it all God delivered him. Yet, the years passed into decades, and Abraham was approaching the century mark. His beautiful wife, Sarah (the Princess), was not many years behind him. Though the promise of God still burned brightly in their hearts, that little son of promise had still not come!

And then, the miracle happened. Strange visitors, heavenly visitors, came to the tents of Abraham at the Oaks of Mamre. Their words were calm, but convincing. "About this time next year you and Sarah shall have a son!" And Sarah, who was listening through the tent curtains, laughed—from joy or sheer amazement—and thereby gave the name to the tiny little one she held in her arms the next year: "Isaac," he was called, for it means "laughter"—and joy flooded their hearts.

Abraham had watched this amazing little one grow. Sometimes the patriarch would lean against the tent pole, to rest his weary old frame, and watch this bundle of perpetual motion. Dashing here—dashing there—Isaac was a wonder to behold. A rock thrown at a wild goat, a mad race to try to catch the desert birds which flocked as near as they dared to the black tents—and sometimes the tears trembled in the eyes of the old patriarch as he marveled at the grace of God: "Indeed, the Lord is good. He keeps his promises; his ways are past finding out. One day, through that lad, the Promised One will come. To God be the glory!"

Then this! Surely God could not be asking this! He had

given this son by a miracle of his grace; would he now take him back and defeat his own purpose? How could Abraham explain this to Sarah? For that matter, how could he explain it to little Isaac?

Did Abraham wonder, as we might have done, if he could be losing his mind? Could the pagan practices of human sacrifice be driving him to this rash deed . . . so Abraham must have struggled in agony of soul to understand and to be absolutely sure of the will of God.

The Bible offers abundant illustration of the fact that only in the deepest agony of personal struggle do we come to know the will of God. Only in our deepest suffering are we able to look into the heart of God . . . who poured out his own life in the suffering of his Son on Calvary. "None of the ransomed ever knew, how deep were the waters crossed . . ."

But Abraham did not haggle or complain. Convinced in his heart of hearts, he arose early in the morning, and, taking the boy and some servants, he made the three-day journey to the foot of Mount Moriah. They pitched their camp that last night in a little valley beneath the mountain, beside a brook that one day would be called the Brook Kidron; and a garden of olive trees would stand one day where they stretched their blankets to rest . . . the garden of Gethsemane.

Early in the morning, as the sun peeped over the eastern mountain, later to be called Mount Olivet, and bathed the rocky slopes of Mount Moriah, Abraham shook the lad awake. Quietly they prepared for the journey to the top. Notice verse six: "And Abraham took the wood of the burnt offering, and laid it upon Isaac his son: and he took the fire in his hand, and a knife; and they went, both of them together."

What a picture is captured by the inspired writer! An old,

gray-headed father and a little boy, on their way up the
mountainside to build an altar and worship God . . . *together*.
Isaac had gone many times with his father; he knew all about
the sacrifice of the burnt offering, and he remembered everything that was needed . . . the *wood* was on his own back . . .
and Daddy had the coals of fire in the bronze bucket, and the
knife was stuck in his belt . . . but something was missing!
The most important thing was *missing* . . .

Abraham could see the question coming, and he wondered
how on earth he could answer it: "Daddy, look! You have
the fire and the knife, and here is the wood on my back. But,
Daddy, where is the *lamb* for the burnt offering?" Indeed,
the *sacrifice itself* was missing . . . or *was* it? In this painful
moment, the light of heaven broke through. Abraham, in the
agony of faith, was granted one fleeting glimpse of the heart
of the eternal God: "My son, God will provide himself a lamb
for a burnt offering." Out of the crisis of his own heart,
Abraham cried out in the simplest words of faith. He knew
God was a God of grace and that he would provide to the
uttermost for man's desperate need. God who had always
provided would not fail him now!

Little Isaac was not slow of wit . . . he could count. He
knew exactly what this meant: there was Daddy, the fire, the
knife, the wood, and . . . *little Isaac!* But Isaac trusted his
father and his father's God. Quietly he went along with Abraham to the brow of the hill. They built the altar. So many
times Isaac had helped his father tug at the big stones and
slide them into place for a simple altar. Perhaps he waited
quietly, looking up into the face of his father, as he crossed
his arms for the leather thongs to be passed around them.
The Scripture says simply that Abraham "bound Isaac his
son, and laid him on the altar upon the wood" (v. 9, KJV).

In the supreme act of faithful obedience, Abraham stretched forth the knife toward heaven, believing that God who had given Isaac by a miracle could raise him from the dead to fulfil his promise. Then came the ringing voice of the angel of the Lord: "Lay not thine hand upon the lad, neither do thou anything unto him: for now I know that thou fearest God, seeing thou hast not withheld thy son, thine only son from me" (KJV). And, looking back, he saw a ram caught by his horns in the thicket . . .

Quickly he cut the bonds which bound his boy, and together they prepared the ram for the burnt offering. Kindling the flame, they knelt beside the altar and watched the smoke of the sacrifice ascending with their prayers to heaven.

Now, come a little closer to that altar . . . and tell me what you see . . . I see a little boy, watching that smoke curling up toward heaven; and, like any little boy, he is probably thinking, "That could have been me! In fact it almost *was* me . . ."

And look at the rapt face of the old patriarch. Tears stream down his cheeks and stand gleaming on his gray beard. How glorious are the ways of the Lord. He truly does provide . . . in ways beyond our deepest understanding, God does provide. The faith of Abraham was vindicated. God himself provided the sacrifice . . .

But I am looking right past the shoulder of Abraham at a skull-shaped rocky hill, which rises just to the north of Abraham's altar on Mount Moriah. I am seeing another day, when another brokenhearted Father was watching his only beloved Son toil up *that* hill . . . with a load of wood on his back . . . a load shaped like an old rugged cross. This one, too, laid down his body upon that rude altar of wood—and they *nailed him there.* No cry escaped his lips: "As a lamb before her shearers is dumb, so he opened not his mouth" (KJV). Lift-

ing up that bloody cross, they dropped it into the hole prepared in the rock to receive it. And, sitting down, they
watched him there . . .

Now, will you come closer to that cross . . . and tell me
what you see? I see the heart of a loving Father outpoured on
Calvary's cross. I see the Lamb slain from the foundation of
the world. As a boy, I cried out, "Father, why didn't you
send those twelve legions of angels and take him down from
that cross? Why did you let him die?" And, one day, standing
in our church at home, convicted of my sins, I heard him
gently say, "I could not save my Son . . . and save you! He
must die that you might live." And to that cross I came,
running . . .

> When I survey the wondrous cross
> On which the Prince of glory died;
> My richest gain I count but loss
> And pour contempt on all my pride!

Yes, what God asked of Abraham, he gave himself—a thousand times over. Because Abraham believed God and offered
his dearest and his best upon the altar, he was able to look
straight into the heart of God. He saw a loving Father who
would provide to the uttermost for his children. Come to
Calvary and "Behold the Lamb of God, which taketh away
the sin of the world" (John 1:29, KJV). But there was no
ram to take his place . . . He must die, if we might live!

And now you have climbed this mountain and looked into
the very heart of the living God. You know that God wanted
. . . not the life of little Isaac, but the heart of that father.
Are you ready to climb your mountain and offer your dearest and your best unto God? Are you ready to take up your
cross and follow him?

III. Analysis

Almost any narrative in the Bible will adapt to this type of presentation. It is important to "set the stage," to delineate the topographical and geographical surroundings, and to fill in enough of the details to give the story life. But it is most important to get inside the feelings and emotions of the central characters and try to feel what they felt.

What Abraham experienced on Mount Moriah could never be reduced to a simple formula: "God is gracious;" or "God is the Provider;" or "Faith never fails." Only as we try to see what he experienced, how he felt, why he acted as he did, can we begin to understand the truth of God which comes with such powerful force through the narrative.

Pitfalls to Avoid

One of the great dangers in the interpretation of the biblical narratives is the old pitfall of "typology." While there are elements of truth in the old typology, it is usually carried to ridiculous lengths by those who become enamored of it. Based upon the typological and allegorical techniques of the ancient scholar, Origen, it has been a fascinating and sometimes bizarre form of biblical interpretation for centuries. It sees in all the biblical events not real happenings, not real persons, but *types* of something or someone else. The seven wells of Beersheba become the "seven virtues" of the life of faith (2 Peter 1:5-7), or the bride of Isaac becomes the type of Christ, or, conversely, Isaac is the "type of Christ" and his bride is really the church. Or, the four men who bore the paralytic upon a pallet to Jesus are really faith, hope, love, and some other virtue. Only the ingenuity of the interpreter limits the outrageous possibilities of this kind of "interpretation."

In the example of Abraham and Isaac, everything depends upon keeping the actual historical identity of the persons involved. It is a literal historical father and a literal historical son who came to a deeper understanding of God in a literal historical event. They are themselves, in their historical time and place, with their level of understanding of the nature of God, placing their faith squarely in God's promise and his unfailing concern for them. If they are simply *types*, they lose their own historical identity, and the event becomes an artificial construction—a stage play, without reality.

On the other hand, it is quite true that all through the Bible this phrase "the Lamb of God" resounds with powerful imagery. The biblical people could never forget what God revealed to Abraham, and they applied this title (like many others) to Jesus. Where there are real historical parallels, it is important to stress them. Where there is fulfilment or enrichment of an Old Testament concept in the New, it would be irresponsible to ignore it. Biblical images which are rooted in the actual historical events of the Old Testament became the indispensable bearers of the revelation of God: the blood of the passover; the sacrificial lamb; the prophet like unto Moses; the priest; and the king. All these, and many more, received their highest meaning and fulfilment in Christ—but they all had their own literal meaning in the actualities of history. To ignore or slight this historical fact is to distort the Scriptures.

There is also the pitfall of the chronic "story-teller." Some people have the gift of story-telling. They could recite the virtues of the letters of the alphabet and keep you hanging on the edge of your seat. But the "you are there" approach described in this chapter is not intended to satisfy the urge to tell a story merely because a story may be more interesting than an abstract discourse. It is intended to re-create an actual historical situation in the minds and hearts of hearers, so that they may have the *opportunity*, at least, of feeling and understanding what the people felt in the original events. It is the attempt to make history contemporary—not so much to roll time backward as to roll it forward—bringing Eden, or Goshen, or Calvary into the present moment.

The theological reason that this is a valid and essential part of the interpreter's task is this: God is one and self-same forever. The nature he revealed to Abraham *is* the nature he revealed on Calvary and the nature he reveals to us today. Calvary *is* contemporary, and the love of Christ is still being poured out for those very ones who crucify him. This is the soundest principle of biblical interpretation which can be propounded, and everything in this method of interpretation should be made to serve it.

Points to Remember

Because this method of interpretation is grounded in the very nature of divine revelation through historical events, it is applicable to almost every event recorded in the pages of the Bible. Naturally, the ones that are most effective are those narratives which give us enough of the detail about the persons and events that they actually come alive before our eyes. Many of the events in the life of Abraham, Isaac, and Jacob provide marvelous opportunities for revelation through actual life situations. The story of Joseph and his brethren is one of the great classics of the Bible and of all literature! Moses, Elijah, David, Isaiah, and a host of others confront God in the crises of their lives; and because we can enter into these poignant episodes with them, we can often feel what they felt. The life of Jesus is the supreme example, and the interpreter who is not deeply moved by the struggle of Jesus in Gethsemane or cannot feel the agony of the cross can surely not be touched by anything. The dynamic life of Paul, Peter, or the others presents an almost limitless opportunity for re-creation of a historical situation into which the listener can enter personally.

These simple points should be kept in mind:

1. The narrative must be read and re-read until it actually lives in the mind of the interpreter. Every detail must be in place, and all of the history and archaeological data available must be brought to bear upon it until it stands out boldly.

2. It must be set in its proper historical context. Only the circumstances surrounding an event can clarify the full meaning of the event, and this history must be clearly traced if the actual happening is to live again.

3. The hearer must not be left as a neutral spectator; he must be called into the center of the action. He is not to be entertained—he is to be *confronted* with the claims of God. From the center of the action, make a direct call for confrontation and response. The interpreter who believes that the Bible is the Word of God for our time and for our lives cannot escape this responsibility. Often it is best to make this confrontation very subtly, but its claim should be inescapable.

4. The whole interpretation is strengthened, and clarified, if the meaning of the event can be related to a central theme of the Bible. Just as it is necessary to set an isolated event in its broadest historical context, it is important to set a revelatory event in the broader context of theological meaning. Biblical events are not strung like beads on a thread so much as they shine forth like the many facets of a single brilliant diamond. They are all about the single glorious reality of

God's love for wayward and rebellious mankind and his persistent search for him in judgment and in grace.

5. Finally, trust the Spirit of God to speak through the story as he has spoken to millions across a thousand generations. That is exactly why the stories are in the Bible. They have gripped and thrilled and challenged men across the ages, and the Word which has come alive in the hearts of millions will come to life again in you.

2

Following the Pattern

I. The Method

Almost every book of the Bible is a collection of different types of literature. Even the most closely woven literary units, such as the letters of Paul, are still interspersed with hymns, quotations, and excursions into secondary themes. A book like the Psalter is obviously a collection of 150 hymns, each following one or more individual themes, and further classified into five separate books of Psalms. In addition, it is possible to classify them more precisely, according to subject, such as messianic psalms, enthronement psalms, or penitential psalms.

Even in the Gospels, where a more or less continuous narrative is followed, the chronological order is interspersed with parables, miracle stories, and pointed sayings of Jesus which certainly circulated independently in an oral form for many years before they were written down in the Gospels. The same is true of the Pentateuch, where the patriarchal narratives, or the tradition of the Exodus was recited orally in the worship centers and in the family circles for generations before it was set down in written form.

This fundamental characteristic of the biblical literature

must be understood if it is to be properly interpreted. And, this fact provides the basic clue to another method of interpretation which we are about to explore. Each of these literary units, which, taken together, form the bulk of our Bible, achieved a particular *form* or *pattern* as it was repeated and repeated in the long period of oral transmission.

Incidentally, a view of scriptural inspiration which begins only with the written text, and does not go back of it to the inspired prophets and apostles who first gave the message orally, is a very inadequate one. God was active in the *oral* transmission of his Word, through inspired prophet and apostle; and he was also active in the community of faith which recognized and preserved these inspired words as Holy Scripture.

Discovering the Pattern

Within each of these separate units of the biblical text, there is usually a pattern which can be discerned by careful study. Some of these are immediately obvious; they jump off the page at a casual glance. Others are more difficult to discover, and some of these involve a complex overlapping of patterns and themes. If we take isolated verses of Scripture and tear them loose from the pattern into which they are woven, they can be used in terribly false and distorted ways.

This is exactly what Satan did in his temptation of Jesus: he quoted and misused the Scriptures by tearing words and verses out of the pattern of meaning in which they were originally found and actually used them in a way which contradicted their true meaning. The number of those biblical interpreters who practice this kind of quotation would be impossible to compute. It constitutes a devastating attack upon the integrity and truth of the Bible, and the damage done by this kind of Scripture quotation is incalculable.

The most important step in discovering the basic pattern is a careful reading of the entire literary unit. Sometimes the length of the unit is difficult to determine, but in most cases it is obvious. For the Psalms it means the entire psalm, and often the psalms immediately before and after, when they form a theme or cultic group. Such a judgment can be made by careful study over a long period of time, or it can be assisted by the careful research of devout scholars who have written the most reliable commentaries. In the Pentateuch or historical books, it requires the reading of the entire narrative surrounding the key person or event. In the Gospels, it involves the whole parable, the whole miracle story, or the entire discourse of Jesus on a particular theme.

A very great danger to be avoided is the tendency to *impose* a pattern upon the text. Many preachers and Bible teachers have pet subjects which they like to talk about. Or, they see a problem in the church with which they want to deal, and they run through the Scriptures trying to find a text on which to hang what they are going to say anyway. In this situation, a pattern is imposed upon the text which really grows out of the needs and desires of the interpreter rather than coming from the text itself.

One way to avoid this danger is to set up a regular order of biblical teaching or preaching and let the applications to current problems grow out of the order of the biblical text— rather than the reverse order. If certain topics or problems are first chosen, and then the Bible is brought in to lend authority and support, it will almost always be misused. A faithful study of the biblical text will also show us what the real problems are and what is most important for us to study. If we choose our topics of concern from the daily newspapers or the latest fads, we may easily spend our time on some subjects which, from the biblical point of view, are not man's deepest needs.

Another important guideline in discovering the basic pattern of a passage of Scripture is to compare it with other patterns disclosed in the same type of literature. If the pattern is consistent with that of similar Scripture texts, it is another piece of evidence which points to the discovery of the original pattern rather than the imposition of one from the outside. Also, it is wise to check several good commentaries to see if different interpreters from different times and places are coming up with the same basic pattern. If so, this is compelling evidence that the pattern is really there in the Scripture and not just an artificial construction.

All other things considered, the simplest pattern which can be found is usually the most reliable. The occurrence of repeated phrases, the emphasis upon a key word or phrase, the echo of a refrain, or deliberate transitions in thought will normally signal the main lines of the pattern. The reason it is so important to discover this pattern is because it was this pattern which gave form and consistency and preserved the text in a long period of oral transmission. Without this pattern it would not have been preserved in the first place, and without this pattern the meaning may be lost.

Patterns can be very monotonous, and sermonic literature is usually the most barren wasteland when it comes to the question of variety in style and organization. All churchgoers have been bored to the stage of numbness by the inevitable three points and a poem of the typical sermon. Fortunately, the Bible offers much more variety in its patterns. In fact, there is an almost infinite variety within the scope of the sixty-six books. The sermons that are recorded in Acts, however, do seem to share that common characteristic of all sermons—three points. Yet, even there, a remarkable variety appears within this framework, and an appeal for response from the hearers forms a frequent climax to the sermon.

Types of Patterns

The simplest pattern can be illustrated by these sermons recorded in the book of Acts. Peter's great sermon at Pentecost begins with an appeal to the Scriptures—the Old Testament has been fulfilled, and the promises of the centuries are now being fulfilled right before the listeners' eyes. Then, a moving and forthright witness is given of the life of Jesus Christ and the way in which the power of God has been revealed in his life. Finally, an urgent call to repentance forms the climax of the sermon. This basic pattern is repeated throughout the sermons of Acts; and, to some extent, this simple outline shapes much of the other New Testament literature, including the Gospels.

Another obvious pattern can be seen in the discourses of Jesus in the Fourth Gospel. In the conversation with Nicodemus, for example, Jesus makes an enigmatic statement ("Ye must be born again"). Nicodemus misunderstands it in a purely literal way and gives Jesus the opportunity to explain its deeper spiritual meaning for all the rest of us who tend to think like Nicodemus.

In the parables there is a somewhat more subtle pattern in which the occasion and the hearers are often described as a prelude to the parable. For example, Jesus "spake this parable unto certain which trusted in themselves that they were righteous, and despised others" (Luke 18:9, KJV). Then, a very familiar scene is sketched in which the hearers are often able to see themselves. Sometimes it is a very painful confrontation, and the Pharisees in particular were so outraged at Jesus' exposure of their hypocrisy that they were determined to kill him. This parabolic pattern can almost always be reduced to one major idea or thrust in a single parable, and it is extremely dangerous to start reading allegorical parallels and secondary ideas into the parables. More often than not this will lead away from the central purpose of the parable and confuse the real meaning.

In the Psalms and other hymns and hymn-fragments which are scattered throughout the Bible, the most clearly defined literary pattern can be seen. It is easy to see why these clear patterns emerge here. They developed a very refined literary form by their liturgical use in the Temple or in general worship. Furthermore, they had to be sung from memory, and it was necessary to have a clear and intelligible pattern in order to recall the words. Also, the measured use of poetic form contributed to a regular meter, an abundant variety of parallelism, and even the use of a repeated formula or refrain.

Because the Psalms present one of the best examples of pattern-interpretation, one of them has been chosen for the illustration in this chapter. Because it is undoubtedly the best known and most universally loved portion of the entire Bible, Psalm 23 has been selected out of the 150 Psalms in the ancient hymnbook of Israel. But, each of the psalms has a pattern, and the variety is almost as great as the number of psalms.

The first Psalm, for example, has a basic twofold structure of the two ways: the way of the righteous and the way of the ungodly. In the wider pattern this psalm is also introductory to the whole psalter and gives us a clue to the entire collection of hymns. Within this twofold pattern there is a step-by-step threefold progression in the pathway of evil. "Blessed is the man that *walketh* not in the counsel of the ungodly, nor *standeth* in the way of sinners, nor *sitteth* in the seat of the scornful" (v. 1, KJV). In the verbs there is a subtle progression on the pathway of evil—from *walking* (the first passing acquaintance with the evil way) to *standing* (a more confirmed involvement with the company of sinners) to *sitting* (the last stage of resignation to the way of evil). There is a parallel progression in the nouns: from the *ungodly* (those who try to live their lives without God at the center) to the *sinners* (those who therefore always miss the mark morally and spiritually) to the *scornful* (those who have become so confirmed and bitter that they not only do nothing good themselves but heap ridicule upon those who try).

There are many other clearly discernible patterns within this basic twofold structure which is so typical of the Psalms. It shows the infinite care with which the Psalms were written, sung, and preserved; and it opens up a gold mine of spiritual treasure for the patient and observant interpreter. From the popular and brilliant expositions of Charles Haddon Spurgeon (*The Treasury of David*) to the highly technical form-critical studies of the great Norwegian scholar, Sigmund Mowinckel (*Psalmenstudien*), the Psalter continues to offer an irresistible challenge to the devout interpreter.

Psalm 23 is so widely loved because it is truly universal in its appeal. It has a beautiful and simple imagery, but its real power is in the fact that the divine Shepherd is portrayed as meeting every physical and spiritual need—now and forever! It is hard to imagine anything more universal than that. It literally speaks to every condition and every need of man, in life or in death, in happiness or in sorrow, in abundance or in want. Let us briefly trace the pattern which moves from the "green pastures" to the "house of the Lord forever."

II. Example: "The Heavenly Shepherd"

The Shepherd Psalm is a jewel of beautiful simplicity. Translated into every language under the sun, it brings its message of childlike trust and hope into the aching hearts of men. It touches every cord of human need and quickens faith, hope, and love in everyone who responds to its universal appeal.

The psalm is attributed to David. It is not difficult to imagine this shepherd lad lying on a Judean hillside on a starry night, with his sheep bedded down around him, as he looks up to the heavenly Shepherd to care for him as he cares for his sheep. The whole day long David has bent every effort to find green pastures for his flock. Even before they pant from thirst, David has already anticipated their need and planned where to bring them to the still waters. Now, when the darkness has fallen, David is still watchful. He is ready to risk his very life to protect them from the wild beast—while they sleep!

This beloved psalm stands in striking relationship to the psalms around it in the hymnbook of Israel. The one immediately before, Psalm 22, is the agonized cry of the righteous sufferer. It plumbs the depths of lonely suffering and lifts the cry for deliverance on the part of the one who has placed all his hopes in God. It is the psalm which welled up in the heart of Jesus in his horrible agony on the cross: "My God, my God, why hast thou forsaken me?" The psalm immediately following the Shepherd's Psalm is a song of triumph. The Lord of hosts enters victoriously into the everlasting doors.

The three psalms, taken together, run the gamut from bitter humiliation to the glorious triumph of faith—and the twenty-third Psalm is the bridge between these extremes. It is the heavenly Shepherd who takes us through the "valley of the shadow of death" to dwell in his house forever!

The structure of this short psalm is as simple as its beautiful language. It is actually twofold. The exact midpoint of the psalm is "the valley of the shadow of death," and it is a clear transition point. The opening three verses sketch in bold and graphic imagery the day-by-day needs which the Shepherd meets. They are the basic needs—food, and water, and physical strength. But they also move quickly to that deepest need of all, the spiritual reality which alone can give meaning to life—the "paths of righteousness."

The opening words of verse 4 signal a crisis. The "valley of deep darkness," as the Hebrew words might be literally translated, calls forth the image of any dark hour in man's pilgrimage upon this earth. It is perfectly proper to turn to this blessed promise in any time of crisis, when faith knows that the heavenly Shepherd is near. But the deepest crisis for every man is that darkest valley of all, and the "valley of darkness" in David's Judean wilderness contained the threat of violent death for every sheep which passed through. In that dark and narrow passageway, the wild beasts lurked. The ultimate meaning of this phrase can never be fulfilled until one has passed through that last dark hour.

The final three verses breathe a heavenly vision. In fact, many of the images cannot even be understood in reference to this physical life alone. They leap the temporal barriers and climax in the house of the Lord *for ever!* It is a psalm of life here—and life hereafter. It is an unbroken song of physical needs that are transcended by yet greater spiritual needs, and no crisis—not even death—can prevent the Shepherd from fulfilling man's last "want." A simple psalm of incredible beauty, it floods the soul with joy until the "cup runneth over." It lifts the eyes up to the Lord, who is my Shepherd!

This twofold pattern of life here, and hereafter—of today, and for ever—is introduced by a short sentence which surely cannot be surpassed in all the Bible for profundity in simplicity. It is another twofold pattern: "The Lord" is the exalted Name which is above every name. It is the covenant name of the Holy God—Yahweh. It was he who led his people out of Egyptian slavery, through the perilous waters of the Red Sea, and into the Promised Land. None other than the great God of this universe—Creator, Redeemer, Sustainer —is *my* Shepherd, David says.

"The Lord" is the majestic title which thunders forth the awesome holiness and transcendence of the Sovereign Ruler of the universe. Yet, when David calls him my Shepherd, he epitomizes the wondrous truth of divine immanence. The Holy One who is so far above and beyond us that we are not worthy to speak his name has come so near and personally to us that we can speak of him most intimately—*my* Shepherd. His majestic highness and his gentle lowliness are both expressed in this brief introductory statement. It is the conjunction of the holiness of God and the love of God, of the Old Testament and the New. It is the message of the Bible in embryo—the precursor of that incredible news that the divine Word became flesh, the Good Shepherd came to give his life for the sheep.

"I shall not want" summarizes the entire psalm. All the rest of the psalm is an explication of this brief sentence. In intensely personal terms David describes the Shepherd's provision for all his wants—physical and spiritual, in times of joy and in times of crisis, now and forever.

Verses 2 and 3 trace in expressive pastoral imagery the divine provision for our needs, ranging from the simplest

physical ones to the profoundest spiritual need. "He maketh
me to lie down in green pastures." This is an abundance of
food which surpasses the wildest dreams of a Judean shepherd. In those barren hills the clumps of grass were few and
far between. No green meadow stretched out anywhere, and
the few sparse blades of grass had to be protected from
trampling hooves. It was unthinkable that these precious
sprigs of green could be squandered as a blanket on which to
lie. But David's vision soars beyond these rocky hills. The
divine Author of such staggering abundance will make his
flock lie down in the carpet of verdant green!

"He leadeth me beside the still waters." David knew what
any shepherd knew, that the only safe place to bring the
sheep to drink was beside the pools of still water. What little
water was available in that arid land rushed down in bouncing
rapids into the deep canyons below. It was suicide for a little
lamb, or even for a wise old sheep, to inch up to those
slippery rocks to slake its thirst. One dislodged stone, one
moss-covered hummock, and the poor sheep would tumble
down the mountainside with the splashing waters.

If it took all day and endless trouble, David would search
out the quiet pool, nestled in a shaded alcove, or trapped on
a gentle plateau, where the wadi paused in its restless descent
to the Dead Sea below. God, too, leads us to those quiet
places, where the still waters run deep, and where we may
even catch a new glimpse of ourselves in the trembling reflection of the deep pool.

"He restoreth my soul." Immediately we think of that
supernatural part of our nature called the soul. But David,
like all Hebrews, thought of physical vitality first when he
mentioned the soul. It is the word for "life," and it speaks of
the zest for living—life with a plus. Of course, it came to have

a deeper spiritual and psychological meaning throughout the biblical usage. However, it never lost the profound truth that modern men are only recently rediscovering. Man is a psychosomatic unit, a body-soul entity. Anything which affects his body affects his soul. A concern for a man's soul involves a concern for his body and his physical needs. Salvation involves the total man—body and soul!

"He leadeth me in the paths of righteousness for his name's sake." This is what life is all about. Life is not mere existence—life is what we live *for*. Here David scores again with the most exalted insight in the simplest words. Life lived for self is always futile. The self-centered life will turn sick and leave a bitter taste in the mouth. It cannot escape the vicious circle of emptiness and self-destruction. Living for self is spiritual suicide. But David has the key—the only key—by which man can escape from this prison cell of self.

The heavenly Shepherd leads us in right pathways for "his name's sake," that is, according to his own personal will for us, rather than our selfish desires. We live for him and not for ourselves. We were made for him and not for ourselves. His name is his *person,* because the Bible had no word in Hebrew or in Greek which is equivalent to our word "person." The "name" carried the content of the person, his will, his purpose, and his possessions. David is saying that we belong to him, even more literally than David's sheep belonged to him; and man's highest fulfilment is to renounce his own ways and follow the heavenly Shepherd in the pathways he has chosen.

Suddenly, this idyllic pastoral scene is shattered by the harshest reality of all. Danger, darkness, and death lie across the pathway of every man. Is the divine Shepherd able to meet this crisis?

In ringing words of triumphant faith David anticipates the

question: "Yes," he says. Especially at this point in man's journey the Shepherd is near. "Yea, though I walk through the valley of the shadow of death, I will fear no evil: for thou art with me." Many interpreters have called attention to the verb "walk." The one who is afraid *runs,* or cowers. The calm and confident one *walks* through. The dark and treacherous valley in the Judean wilderness, which doubtless gave this image to David, was called the "valley of the shadow of death." It was well named. Death lurked there. A fearful shepherd would hurry his flock through to lessen the mortal danger.

But, the confident walk of faith is unshaken, because the heavenly Shepherd is near. Even the preposition *through* is a remarkable expression of assurance. We do not go blindly into this valley—faith knows that the Shepherd will lead all the way through. In repeated words which are almost shocking in their intimacy with the Holy God, David keeps saying *"I* will fear no evil; for *thou* art with *me."* Not some remote Ground of Being, not some Prime Mover of Aristotelian logic, not some distant Allah is this—but the most intimate, personal God, the Shepherd of the soul. It is the glorious gospel —God so loves *me* that he comes to *me* and cares for *me.*

"Thy rod and thy staff they comfort me." Much debate has been conducted on the exact form and function of the rod and the staff. One thing is fairly certain. It was a single instrument, or at least two ends of a single shaft, which served a double function. It could beat and it could bless. In the hand of the shepherd, the sturdy staff could fend off the attacking wolf or it could rap the cantankerous ram. It could divide the flock at the sheepfold, or the crook could reach gently down to rescue a lamb upon the precipice. Discipline and blessing are in the Shepherd's hand, and his love is expressed as surely when he lifts the chastening rod as when he lifts up the fallen lamb.

"Thou preparest a table before me in the presence of mine enemies." No words in all the psalm are more often misunderstood. This is not some banquet table prepared by the sumptuous hand of the Lord where one may gloat over his enemies. It can be understood only by recalling the familiar "law of refuge" in David's land. When one fled for his life from his enemies, he had only one hope. Even if he had killed or injured someone quite accidentally, he might be cornered like a wild animal and brutally maimed or killed under the primitive law of "an eye for an eye, and a tooth for a tooth." His only hope was to find his desperate way to the home of a friend. Once he crossed the threshold of that tent or dwelling, no violent hand dared reach across to harm him. All the law of the nation or the clan rose up to protect him in the house of his friend. The frustrated enemies might sit and glower beyond the threshold of the tent, or the doorway of the dwelling, but they were powerless to interrupt the feast of honor in the home of a friend.

David is saying that the old enemies of sin, and suffering, and death may pursue him all the way to the threshold of the house of the Lord—but they cannot enter there! He has found eternal refuge at the table of the Lord.

"Thou anointest my head with oil." There is nothing in this picture that is very appealing to the typical modern man. The idea of a fragrant oil being poured upon the head until it runs down the face or beard is not altogether pleasing. But, in David's day, it would have been the supreme delight—because of what it *meant!* Virtually every family, even some very poor ones, would make almost any sacrifice to keep this treasure upon the shelf at home. A box or jar of precious oil would be reserved for that special moment, that surpassing occasion, when the family wanted to express its highest love and honor. The person who received this tender expression of affection was signally honored. For a poor family it might represent a real financial sacrifice, but the significance of the act far surpassed any monetary value placed upon the gift.

David was making the astounding assertion that in the Shepherd's home, at the banquet table of the Lord, he was made the welcome guest. The Lord delighted to do him honor—with the oil of anointing he owned him as his special guest. And the overflowing cup was but the final gracious act which confirmed the genuineness of the welcome. When the host filled the cup to overflowing, it was a sign of overflowing joy at the presence of the guest. A cup half-filled could be an oriental invitation to leave. David's host left no doubt—the overflowing cup portrayed an overflowing welcome.

"Surely goodness and mercy shall follow me all the days of my life . . ." Some interpreters have seen in this a continuation of the shepherd imagery. Just as the faithful shepherd dogs follow and herd the flock into the sheepfold, so goodness and mercy herd the spiritual sheep into the heavenly fold. Whether this direct imagery is intended or not, the truth is clear: with goodness and mercy the heavenly Shepherd will guide and protect his flock along every step of life's journey. A wandering sheep could never go so far or lag so far behind that he would escape the persistent goodness and mercy of the Lord. The man who chooses the broad road to destruction will do so by stubborn defiance of this pursuing love and grace—to the last breath.

"And I will dwell in the house of the Lord forever." Some interpreters have made gratuitous remarks about correcting the translation to "I shall," since *shall* is normally used with the first personal pronoun and *will* with the second and third. One can occasionally hear a reader of this beloved psalm make this obvious "correction" without knowing what he is doing. The translators of the familiar version were faithfully preserving the force of David's words. They reflect strong certainty—an unshakable faith—and when *will* is used with the first person, that is exactly what it means. With resounding assurance David affirms his faith. He *knows* whom he has believed, and he is sure that he will dwell "in the house of the Lord for ever."

There are some who have tried to limit this phrase "the house of the Lord" to the physical Temple in Jerusalem and who argue that it can mean no more than the desire of a devout Israelite to stay in the Temple forever. To be more explicit, it would, in that case, have to refer to camping out in one of the courtyards, since neither the Holy Place or the holy of holies, or even the court of the priests would be available to David. Such literalism applied consistently to this psalm would be nonsense indeed. It would portray people literally lying around in green pastures, or drinking at deep pools, or being chastened by a club.

To dwell in the house of the Lord means to be in the presence of the Lord forever. It means unbroken communion with the One whom not having seen we love. It means that after the long and dangerous journey we are *home* at last—the home for which we were made. It means the fulfilment of the deepest, the highest, the holiest longings which the divine Shepherd has placed in our hearts. It means to be face to face with him—*forever*. Can heaven be more than that?

So there it is—the most universally loved and cherished passage in all the writings in all the languages in all the long history of man. Remarkable in its simplicity, but powerful in its haunting images which linger in the heart, it speaks to men of faith, in times of joy, or the hour of deepest sorrow. And small wonder—for in its brief six verses it sweeps the whole range of human longing, from the earthiest needs of the physical appetite to the highest fulfilment of the devout spirit—eternal fellowship with the living God! It is the ultimate expression of the pathway of faith. There is only one twenty-third Psalm. There can never be another. Until our faith has become sight—until that valley has been traversed and the heavenly dwelling is complete—we can never come nearer than we do through the words of the Shepherd Psalm!

III. Analysis

The use of the literary pattern which is integral to the Scripture passage itself was very direct and explicit in the example just given. Sometimes it may be wise to spell out clearly the outline or pattern which is being followed. At other times it may be followed by the interpreter without explicit reference to it in the sermon or Bible lesson. In any case, it should not be allowed to obscure the words of the Scriptures themselves or to detract from the message of the text. That would be rather like an X-ray picture of the skeleton displacing a portrait of the living person. For the pattern is just that—it is a skeleton, a framework, upon which the living body is supported, and by means of which it moves. It is as essential to the form and movement of the text as the skeleton is to the form and movement of the body; but without the breath and sinews, it is just a stack of bones.

In selecting those Scriptures which are best interpreted by means of a pattern, it is wise to consider these points:

1. The poetic passages of the Bible are the prime examples of a literary pattern. This includes all the Psalms, many of the

oracles of the prophets (which are printed in poetic form in all modern translations), the hymns and hymn-fragments in the letters of Paul (such as the "Hymn of Love" in 1 Cor. 13), the ancient songs of Moses, Miriam, Deborah, and all the rest. In all these the pattern has been carefully woven throughout the passage. Poetry is nothing without a pattern; and while it can be enjoyed for sound and imagery without dissecting the pattern, it can never be really understood until that key unlocks it. Psalm 23 can be read and enjoyed just for its words, its images, and its sounds. But, only by unfolding the pattern can its deepest truth be disclosed.

2. While the narrative passages are not the best subjects for the pattern approach, many of them do show a clearly defined pattern, especially in a series such as the patriarchal narratives, the Joseph stories, the Elijah-Elisha stories, and other such groups. Often, the pattern is secondary in these, and a pattern approach might be used to supplement the more direct "you are there" approach described in chapter 1.

3. The reason for going to almost any length of study and effort to discover the pattern is this: it is through the form and pattern that the meaning has been preserved down through the centuries, and only the recovery of this pattern can unlock that meaning. The literary art is like any art. Form and style are not incidental to the meaning of the poem, the painting, or the symphony—they are the bearers of the meaning. Anyone who really cares will pay the price to understand the form and structure which speak so eloquently.

The "pattern approach" is only one method of interpreting the Scriptures. It is not always appropriate, and it can sometimes be misused. But one decisive fact remains: for the many portions of Scripture which are clearly distinguished by a literary pattern or structure, it is the one best means of unlocking the meaning. For anyone who really cares about that message and who wants to open it up for others, the search for the pattern is of absolute importance. Upon that literary "skeleton" the body of the Word lives and moves!

3

Developing the Theme

I. The Method

One of the most exciting ways of studying any piece of literature is to search for the sometimes elusive theme which runs throughout the writing and which gives unity and purpose to the whole. It can be exciting because it contains the possibilities of a piece of detective work. A clue here and a link there may begin to fall in place to reveal the real motive for the writing.

Sometimes the theme is stated plainly upon the face of the work, and in these cases it should be a simple matter to follow and develop the theme. However, it is never simple. There are almost always secondary themes underlying the major one, and sometimes these are more important and revealing than the obvious one. This is exactly like another artistic creation—the symphony. A major theme may come to the surface again and again, but often the secondary or counterthemes receive more attention and may give immortality to the whole work.

In simplest terms, a method of interpretation which attempts to "develop the theme" will involve these steps:

1. Repeated reading of the entire literary unit will usually

51

open up the major theme or purpose of the writing.

2. A careful, verse-by-verse study of the text will then show how each sentence contributes to the development of that theme. It can also provide an important check upon the accuracy of the definition of the theme. If the individual verses fail to confirm and support the major theme, something is wrong. Either the theme has not been correctly defined, or the individual verses are not being correctly interpreted.

3. The real value of the method depends upon a third step: each new sentence or paragraph must add something to the major theme—that is, it must develop the theme. This step is all-important for the interpreter. Meaning is always bound up with *relationships*. If something is absolutely isolated it has no meaning. In fact, anything which is absolutely isolated could not be observed or known in the first place. But if the interpreter can trace the steps by which each verse or paragraph builds up the theme, he has opened up a breadth of meaning which cannot be discovered in any other way.

4. Finally, the method must vindicate itself by completing the "circle of meaning." It is the theme or purpose in the mind of the author which gives coherence to the writing. Every single verse, and even every single word, was called into use for the purpose of developing and communicating that theme. Only when the interpreter has worked all the way back to this purpose of the author, and is literally thinking his thoughts after him, has the communicative process been completed.

Thematic Passages in the Bible

As in the case of the other methods, the thematic approach could be of some value in interpreting almost any passage of Scripture. Any paragraph or composition which makes sense at all must have some purpose or meaning. But there are certainly some portions of the Bible which are more dependent upon this type of elucidation than others.

The letters of the New Testament are the primary examples of this thematic writing. Often, there is more than one theme disclosed in the course of an epistle; but there is usually a dominant concern or problem which prompted the letter in the first place. The Gospels are also very thematic, and the use of the materials in differing ways by the four Gospel writers is conclusive evidence of the overriding importance of the primary theme or themes they are developing. This is the clue to the interpretation of the Gospels in the best of modern scholarship. The evangelist employs or excludes certain material, and even arranges its order or setting, in such a way as to reinforce his purpose in writing. This fact is the most obvious conclusion of a century of historical research in the Gospels, and it would be a tragedy to ignore the light this sheds upon these precious documents of the Christian faith.

All of the individual oracles of the prophets reflect one or more themes, and even the entire books of the major and minor prophets should be interpreted in the light of the central themes. The Psalms are also thematic, and the literary sources of the Pentateuch (the priestly editor, the Deuteronomist, the Yahwist, *etc.*) are defined as clearly by their theme as by their language and style. The Apocalypse is also a prime example, not only because it contains letters addressed to particular situations, but because it is the most notable expression of the major apocalyptic themes and symbols which echoed throughout postexilic Judaism and early Christianity.

Defining the Theme

If this method is to be employed successfully, great care must be taken in defining the theme. The scope of the literary unit is an integral part of the definition of the theme. If one reads 1 Corinthians 13, he could certainly maintain that its theme is *love*. If he reads chapter 11, he might argue that the theme is the abuse of the Lord's Supper or how to correct it. If he reads chapter 14, he would be bound to say that the theme is the misuse of tongues in public worship and how to correct it.

A broader reading of the entire Epistle of 1 Corinthians, however, would give a more comprehensive theme into which these sub-themes fit. Paul is dealing with questions which have been addressed to him in a letter, and the common thread which ties them together is the problem of division and dissension which has arisen in the church at Corinth. In the light of his overall purpose, it is possible to interpret each chapter and each paragraph as Paul's attempt to overcome this shameful conflict within the fellowship and show the Corinthians how to achieve the reality of the one body in Christ, with all the diversity of the gifts and functions of the various members of the body. The discovery of this master theme throws light on all the Epistle and helps to avoid the serious misinterpretation of a single paragraph or chapter which has been taken out of this context.

The powerful truth in this method of interpretation is this: there is an underlying unity in Christian truth, in the church, in the meaning of baptism and the Lord's Supper, and in the life which triumphs over the grave. Only in its relationship to him in whom all things cohere, in relationship to Jesus Christ, does any Christian truth have value or meaning. The discovery and definition of this relationship is the key to the "thematic" approach. It is the properly *theological* method of interpretation, because it relates each paragraph or chapter to the theme of the whole book, and this theme to the whole of the Christian faith. Anyone who has ever studied carefully the whole of the Bible, in all of its diversity of language and subject and culture across many centuries, cannot but stand in absolute awe of the powerful unity and coherence of its central message. It is a compelling argument for the inspiration of the writing, because such unity is a surpassing miracle. Confused and contradictory men could never have produced such a work. The Bible displays unity in diversity; but it never gives us two gods, or two moral standards, or two ways of salvation, or two definitions of reality. It is powerfully and persuasively *one* in its central message. This can be accounted for in only one way—its ultimate Author is the *One Holy God!*

II. Example: "The Marks of a Christian"

The little first letter of John was written almost nineteen centuries ago, and yet there is no line in today's newspaper which is more relevant or "up-to-date." It is also intensely personal. It could not be more personal if it had been addressed to you by name and dropped into your mailbox this morning. It is a word straight from the Eternal into the here and now—and it can transform your life. Are you willing to give a few moments of your undivided attention to hear this word which God has spoken down through the centuries, and which he is speaking to you right now?

John leaves no doubt about his purpose in writing. He spells it out: "These things have I written unto you that believe on the name of the Son of God; that ye may know that ye have eternal life, and that ye may believe on the name of the Son of God" (5:13, KJV). Throughout the entire letter, this is clearly his purpose. He wants his readers to *know* that they have eternal life. He wants them to *know* that they are believing on the name (that is, the *person*) of the Son of God, and not on something else. Everything in the letter is designed to test and confirm this saving relationship to Christ. Nothing could be more important.

In some ways, this letter is even more urgent today than it was when John wrote it. There is more confusion today about what it means to be a Christian than there has ever been. More people are fearful and uncertain about God, or their relationship to him, than the world has ever seen. How relevant is this letter! Do you know where you stand? Do you know that you have passed out of death into life? Do you know that Christ is your Saviour and that through faith you can overcome the world? Listen prayerfully for just a few moments to John's words—and you will *know!* Anyone can know. Everyone *must know,* because salvation is not a problematic or uncertain thing. It is the most certain and positive reality in life. Assurance is its very essence, and the mark of the new life in Christ is the overwhelming certainty of his presence.

How do you know? John spells out the answer in one, two, three fashion. "That which was from the beginning, which we have heard, which we have seen with our eyes, which we have looked upon, and our hands have handled, of the Word of life" (1:1). John is describing a personal experience with the Lord. To be sure, he had seen Jesus in the flesh. He had known him as a man among men. This might seem to give John an advantage in knowing Jesus as the living Lord; but, the truth is, it was probably much harder for John to believe in Jesus as the Son of God than it is for us!

We know Christ in the Spirit as the risen, living Saviour. John met him, first, simply as a man walking beside the Sea of Galilee. But for us, as for John, there has to be a time when we come to meet Jesus in direct, personal experience. He must be as real for us as our own life—no secondhand experience will do. One cannot be saved by relying on the minister's faith, or the creed of the church. The beliefs of the parents cannot be passed on to the children like a family heirloom. Everyone must meet Jesus for himself, in a genuine personal experience. The reality of his daily presence in your life must be as certain as the breath in your body and the blood in your veins. Do you know the Lord Jesus in a vital, personal relationship? No one is a Christian unless he has this deep, personal assurance that he has met Christ and that Christ is living in him. Paul joins with John in declaring this fundamental fact of the Christian life: "I am crucified with Christ; nevertheless I live; yet not I, but Christ liveth in me" (Gal. 2:20, KJV).

But John goes on to paint the picture still more clearly: "That which we have seen and heard declare we unto you, that ye also may have fellowship with us" (1 John 1:3). What John experienced with Jesus, he had to share with others— because the life in Christ is *made* for fellowship. We cannot keep it to ourselves. Every genuine Christian shares his faith in Christ with others; the glow of his Christian joy touches everyone he meets. The new life in Christ can never be experienced at the deepest level until it is shared with others.

I remember coming home and finding my little son with a terrible case of the mumps. I felt great sympathy for him, but I did not worry much about myself. After all, it is a "child's disease" (I thought), and I had it when I was a boy (I thought). But, in about two weeks, I came down with the most horrible case of the mumps you ever saw. My swollen jaws made an almost perfect triangle from the top of my head to each shoulder. People actually went into hysterics when they saw me.

Do you think I could blame this little son for giving me the mumps? Of course not. It is a contagious disease, and anyone who has a good case is going to be sharing it with everyone he meets. That is the nature of anything contagious—when you get near it, you are likely to catch it.

So it is with Christianity! When someone has a good case of the love of Christ in his heart, he is contagious. Anyone who is near him is liable to catch it. Quite literally, you cannot keep Christ to yourself. As one popular song puts it, "Love isn't love until you give it away!"

Some people think it is only the preacher or the missionary who has the responsibility of witnessing for Christ and leading others to know him. The truth is—every Christian must be a soul-winner. He does not have to *drive* himself to it. If he is a genuine Christian, he cannot help it. He could no more avoid witnessing for Christ than he could stop breathing. It is his very nature to share the greatest experience he has ever known—personal fellowship with Jesus Christ. How long has it been since you went directly to a friend or neighbor to share your Christ with him? If you are not witnessing for him and continuously seeking to lead others to your Saviour, there is something desperately wrong with your Christian life. It may be that you are afraid to talk to others about Jesus because you are not sure that you know him yourself. A deep yearning to share Christ with others is one of the clearest signs of the Christian life.

John continues his theme in verse 8 of chapter 1: "If we

say that we have no sin, we deceive ourselves, and the truth is not in us." What a surprising turn this takes! Christians and church members like to think of themselves as the good people, people who would not do some of the things that other people do. There is even the subtle danger that a religious person can begin to think that he may be a little better than some other people he could name.

But, strange as it may sound, a real Christian is the first one to admit that he is a sinner. He is not always trying to justify himself and prove that he is right. The unbeliever will nearly always begin to explain that he is really a very good person, or that he has never done anything very bad. Usually he will point to someone in the church and claim that he is a lot better than that sorry hypocrite! You see, the attitude of the unbeliever is exactly this—he is trying to justify *himself* before God, as Jesus said of the Pharisee. He is trying to trust his own goodness, and therefore he has to be very self-righteous in his own sight.

The true Christian knows that he has been forgiven much, and he can never be self-righteous about his life. Only by God's forgiving grace can anyone be saved. The closer one lives to Christ, the more he is aware of his own sinfulness and unworthiness. When Isaiah was very near to the Lord in a glorious experience in the Temple, he cried out, "Woe is me! for I am undone; I am a man of unclean lips . . ." (Isa. 6:5). When Paul, the prince of the apostles, looked at his own life, he did not extol his goodness. He said, "I am the chief of sinners" (1 Tim. 1:15). This is always characteristic of the true Christian. Because of his very nearness to God, he is aware of his sinfulness. Because of his constant dependence upon the forgiving grace of God, he feels the need of continual confession. When you feel deeply unworthy of his love and long to have your soul cleansed of every stain—rejoice! It is the clearest sign of God's Spirit working in your heart. It is the genuine mark of a child of God!

Now, brace yourself for the acid test. John knew exactly where we live in the midst of this sinful world. He knew where the hardest challenge to Christian living would be met. In 1 John 2:9 (KJV), he drives to the heart of the matter: "He that saith he is in the light, and hateth his brother, is in darkness even until now." No one ever said it better. If you are carrying hatred in your heart toward another, you are still in the outer darkness. John even says that you cannot have in the same heart love toward God and hatred toward a fellow-man (4:20)! No matter what his race, or background, or condition—and no matter what he may have done—a Christian cannot hate him. A Christian will always forgive.

This is such a demanding challenge that some people throw up their hands in despair. Who then can be a Christian? It is important to remember that John is not referring simply to some disagreement between brethren. We may often see things differently—Paul and Peter did. John is not even referring to a loss of temper, sinful as that may be. The Bible says, "Let not the sun go down upon your wrath!" Rather, he is referring to that rancoring bitterness in the heart, which comes from some hurt or misunderstanding, and the attitude of unforgiving hatred which festers there. Is there anyone in this world against whom you bear this kind of bitterness?

Once a woman rushed up to me after I had preached on this text and caught me by the coat lapels and just shook me, like a naughty schoolboy! She screamed at me, "If you just knew what that woman did to me, you'd hate her too!" Of course, I had no idea who the woman was, or what someone had done to her—but I had to ask, "Did she nail you to a cross? . . . Did she push a crown of thorns down upon your brow? They did that to our Lord, and he prayed, 'Father, forgive them.' ... And, by his grace, every child of his will forgive, too." If you harbor bitterness or hatred against another—if you cannot forgive, you are giving a graphic demonstration of the fact that you have not been forgiven. Every true Christian will forgive because Christ has forgiven him!

John scales a spiritual mountain peak in chapter 2, verse 15: "Love not the world, neither the things that are in the world. If any man love the world, the love of the Father is not in him." From this lofty point, John is actually surveying the whole of the Christian life. It is a key idea in his letter. He is saying that everything in the Christian life is determined by this one question: what is your *first love?* Most Christians would be quick to answer, "Christ!" But the real answer is found in another way. What do you talk about the most? What do you think about the most, in the very depths of your heart? What do you plan to do with your time and energy? What do you really *give yourself* to? This is your *first* love, no matter what your words may say. Does Christ claim this place in your life? He will not accept any other. ...

In verse 16 John points out that for some people the first place belongs to the lust of the flesh, the desire for sensual gratification. Sex, or drink, or the desire to "live it up" becomes their god. For some, it is the "lust of the eyes," the desire to have that which is pleasing to the aesthetic tastes. Material possessions can easily become an end in themselves —idols which claim the mind, the energies, and the soul. For many others, it is the pride of life—the will to have one's own way, to live life without taking God into account ... or *anyone* else! This is the supreme idolatry—to try to live without God.

Every Christian knows that there are those who have declared their faith in Christ and entered the Christian fellowship with such great promise—only to turn their backs upon it and bring reproach upon the name they have confessed. John does not shrink from facing this tragic problem. Although some may say they were temporarily saved, and then lost, John knows better. They are antichrists because they never truly belonged to Christ. "They went out from us, but they were not of us; for if they had been of us, they would no doubt have continued with us: but they went out, that they might be made manifest that they were not all of us" (2:19, KJV). Steadfast discipleship is the grand mark of the Christian. All his profession, prayers, and service are nothing if he does not demonstrate his oneness with Christ by faithful perseverance.

What is the mark of a Christian? *Endurance*—faithful, unswerving loyalty to Jesus Christ. A faith that will not endure is a faith that cannot save. How many are the church members who seem to be placing their hope in a profession once made—in the fact that they walked down an aisle one time, many years ago. The question is not how emotional or how dramatic was an experience of the long ago—the question is, how faithful are you to Christ now? John draws the line: if you turn away from fellowship with Christ and his people, you have never really belonged to him!

We may well conclude this study of the Christian life by looking at the verse which summarizes the whole letter. It carries to fullest expression the Christian characteristics described in the first two chapters. "We know that we have passed from death unto life, because we love the brethren" (3:14). There is no higher way than love. Sometimes people can claim to be defenders of orthodox doctrine, but show by their contempt for the fellowship of the brethren that they do not belong to Christ. Sometimes others can pride themselves on a rigid and strict moral standard, and yet be so mean and evil-spirited that they cannot get along with any-body.

It was said of early Christians: "Behold, how they love one another!" Is this the mark of our churches today? Are Christians known for the love and fellowship which bind them together? Tragically, some church groups are known more for their fighting and squabbling than for their fellowship. The Christian is known by his *love*—his love for Christ, and his love for others!

This is the theme of a little letter that reaches down across the centuries to quicken new life within us. Every verse of the letter could be traced to show this one purpose: that we may *know* that we have this eternal life in Jesus Christ. How do you measure up? All of us know about the rigors of a thorough physical examination. John has given us a soul-stretching examination of our relationship to Jesus Christ. He has given us a picture of our spiritual condition.

Do you pass?

1. Have you met Jesus Christ *personally?*

2. Do you share him with others?

3. Do you confess your sins, or do you think that you are always right?

4. Is there someone you cannot forgive?

5. Has something else claimed first place in your life?

6. Are you faithfully serving Christ, today, or have you wandered away?

7. Do you love the fellowship of the brethren? When you answer these questions you will *know* whether you are his.

III. Analysis

Such a theme-study as this is appropriate for a single chapter, or a few verses, or even for the entire book. Sometimes, as in this case, a selection of verses which develop the theme

is all that can be covered in a single period. This can be even
more effective when each verse is carefully chosen for its
distinctive contribution to the theme.

In the light of the example just given, these points should
be kept in mind:

1. The overall theme must be related to the whole body of
Christian truth, preferably in the opening paragraphs of the
interpretation. This is important because it validates the significance of the theme as a whole and it shows how each
point of the interpretation is related to the Christian life as a
whole.

2. Each successive point of interpretation must clearly
show what is being added to the total theme of the writing.
In other words, interpretation is not just a series of running
comments on Bible verses. It is the exposition of the meaning
of each verse in relation to the whole; and it culminates in
the application of their meaning to the Christian life today. If
each point does not add something *new* to the development
of the theme, the method is failing in its purpose.

3. The transition from point to point or verse to verse
should be made explicitly so that the hearer is looking for the
new idea which is being added to the total theme. He should
not be left in doubt by a too subtle or indirect style. If the
hearer misses the point that is being made, he should at least
know that he has missed it. He should not be left wondering
whether the interpreter was trying to make one.

4. The development of the theme should be kept moving.
If it drags, it will die in your hand. Some of the old exposi-
tors would circle round and round the same text and the
same point until the listener wanted to gnaw on a file. It is
doubtful that this was ever an effective form of communica-
tion. Today it is absolutely impossible, because listeners are

geared to movement. If it does not move, they quit. Leave each point before it—and the audience—are exhausted; and be sure that the next one adds a new dimension.

A Variety of Applications

This thematic method can be applied in many different ways, and it can accomplish what no other method of interpretation can.

For example, it is the ideal way of dealing with doctrinal subjects in the Scriptures. With a careful use of a topical index or concordance, the theme of baptism, or repentance, or any other doctrine may be traced through the sacred writings. Such a survey might cover the whole Bible, or it might be restricted to Paul's letters, or to the prophets, or any other grouping of the biblical literature.

The theme approach is also very effective in *comparing* the biblical writings. One of the most instructive ways of studying the Gospels, for instance, is to compare their themes and see how the different evangelists develop their various emphases. An analysis of the various themes of the Psalms will open up an exciting new understanding of the history, the theology, and the worship patterns of Israel. Comparing the themes of Paul's various letters will throw light upon his life situation and help to establish the order and relationship of the writings.

The theme-approach is perhaps most valuable in its contribution to the theological development of the Christian. Literally thousands of Christians have heard sermons and Bible lessons on verses, chapters, and books, and yet do not have any comprehensive understanding of the whole body of Christian truth. They may never have an opportunity to see anything in relation to the totality of the Christian life.

Young people of today often have a terrible caricature of Christian doctrine in their minds because they have received an idea here and a point there, and they have never been required to see the whole body of Christian truth in its inter-relationship. The thematic approach will do more than any other to show these relationships and fill out the whole pic-ture of the Christian faith. Without it the Christian may be stumbling along blindly, led into every weird and distorted doctrine which crosses his pathway.

Evaluation

Something like this thematic approach ought to be the "stock-in-trade" of every preacher and Bible teacher. It is the staple of the spiritual diet, and without it spiritual anemia will develop.

Every Christian doctrine ought to be studied throughout the Bible by following the theme through both Testaments and all the major literary divisions. Every book of the Bible should be approached and analyzed to discover its theme or themes.

Only out of such a comprehensive study of the whole Bible can any interpreter ever come to the place that he can interpret each passage in the best possible context—the con-text of the whole message of the Bible. For this reason, every young minister or Bible teacher ought to major on this type of Bible study, in order to build the background necessary for a lifetime of interpretation. Only out of this broad back-ground of devoted study can the interpreter bring the Word alive for his hearers today.

4

Applying the Principle

I. The Method

The most obvious problem in interpreting the Bible is the fact that all of it was written about people and circumstances thousands of years ago. Try to imagine how many writings in the field of science, or medicine, or music, are still being used after two or three thousand years! The number is so small and the irrelevance of those ancient writings is so great that it is simply ridiculous. Yet, every day, in all parts of the world, men are taking the ancient words of the Bible and are trying to apply them to the life situations of today. Of course, the only reason a man will do this is because he is convinced that the Bible is different from other ancient writings—that it is uniquely inspired by God's Holy Spirit—and that its ancient message is still the Word of God in our time and place.

There is only one way that such a practice can be maintained. We are convinced that underneath the words of Scripture—addressed to Corinth, or to the Israelites in Egypt, or to the Christians in Rome—may be found eternal principles which are true and valid today for men in the Congo, or Chicago, or the plains of Tibet. We hold the steadfast assurance that although the faces, the customs, and the historical circumstances change, the basic truth of God does not change. Men still are sinners who need to be called back from their rebellion into obedience and faith in God. The sacrificial love of God revealed in the cross of Christ is still speaking its eternal message of divine sacrifice and forgiveness through the words and deeds of those who have taken up their cross to follow Jesus.

Almost all who love and accept the Bible believe that it is the eternal message of God—but they divide into a thousand camps when it comes to the question of how to interpret that message and apply it to our lives today. This chapter is an attempt to show the main steps which are involved in the tremendous task of discovering the eternal principles which underlie the historical message and events of the Bible. Then, by example and explanation, those principles will be applied to the changed historical circumstances of our day. This is a difficult and dangerous task, but every interpreter of the Word is called upon to attempt it. Only as we trust the Holy Spirit to guide us as he guided the ancient writers can we hope for success.

From the Shell to the Kernel

It would be possible to list hundreds of examples of specific biblical injunctions and commandments which either have no meaning today or would be absolutely contradictory to the prevailing message of the Bible if they were carried out literally. Not many people today are faced with the agony of deciding whether to boil a kid in its mother's milk, or exactly how to paste a written prayer on the forehead, or where to find meat for sale which has not been sacrificed to idols. These matters, and a hundred others, were critical issues for the biblical people; but they do not apply directly to anything which modern man is experiencing. Yet, underneath the shell of the historical circumstances can usually be found that kernel of eternal truth which speaks to men of every generation in their own peculiar circumstances.

An example or two will help to clarify this claim that an eternal principle underlies these very specific, and sometimes strange, injunctions to men of old:

1. Paul, for example, plainly commands the women to keep silence in the churches (1 Cor. 14:34). He also requires that a woman's head be covered and that her hair be kept long as a natural covering which is her glory (11:5-15). There are still earnest people who try to carry out the very letter of these scriptural words, without having any idea in the world what kind of historical situation Paul was facing or what he was talking about. In their slavish obedience to the literal words, they are actually falling into a practice today which absolutely contradicts what Paul intended.

These words were addressed to the believers in Corinth. In the midst of that wicked city stood the mountain called "Acrocorinth," a rugged bluff upon which the Temple of Aphrodite was built. This pagan goddess of sex was worshiped and served by a thousand female prostitutes, who plied their ancient trade upon the streets of Corinth below. With uncovered head, and brazen directness, they would approach and speak to men, whether singly or in groups in the streets and marketplaces of the city. A chaste woman simply would not behave in this way. Such appearance, and such bold speaking in the presence of men, was the very badge of a scandalous profession.

Now, it is clear that in such a situation, any woman who displayed herself in this way, or immodestly raised her voice in public assembly, or even drew attention to herself, was in danger of being identified with this professional group of pagan harlots. From his words and from the historical situation in Corinth, we can tell what the issue was for Paul. The Christian women simply must not conduct themselves in any way which might confuse them with such evil women, and they should at all times act and dress in such a way as to show modesty and reflect honor upon the name of Christ. Spelled out in this way, we have a principle which is as valid in the twentieth century as in the first—and one which is very much needed in any century.

It is important to remember that such principles, stated in abstract terms, can only be found in textbooks. In real life, they are confronted in actual situations, just like the one Paul faced at Corinth. A principle is never significant in abstract definition—it must be applied to a specific situation before it has real meaning.

2. Another example, from the words of Jesus, will help to illustrate the point. In the Sermon on the Mount, Jesus is dealing with the Pharisees' hypocrisy in the matter of taking oaths. They were guilty of such duplicity that—if they could make a promise, without taking a certain kind of oath—they felt no obligation to fulfil their word. Even if an oath were exacted from them, they would try to devise an oath which had a loophole in it, so that they could avoid keeping it.

In such a situation as this, it could be assumed that a man would probably be lying to you, unless you put him on oath. And, if you put him on oath, it was very likely that the oath was deceptive anyway. No wonder Jesus condemned this with such scathing words. His point was that men should always tell the truth—whether they are under oath or not! One should not even have to take an oath to guarantee his veracity. His *yes* should always mean *yes,* and his *no* should mean *no*.

When people today make such an issue of an oath of allegiance to the flag or to defend the nation, they are dealing with something entirely different. Jesus was talking about vows which these legalists had made to pay a certain amount to the Temple, or on an individual debt, only to begin immediately to find some way to wiggle out of the responsibility of fulfilling the commitment. Today, when people haggle about the pledge of allegiance to flag or nation, they are engaging in almost exactly the same kind of legalistic casuistry and dodging of responsible commitment which Jesus was condemning in the Pharisees. The attitudes involved are almost identical. It is a tragic fact that the literal words of the Bible can be taken out of the historical situation of the first century and applied *directly* to the twentieth, in such a way that they absolutely contradict the meaning in the Bible. This is why the discovery of the *principle* is so important. Once discovered, it can be properly applied in any century.

The principle, in this case, is literally shouting from the pages of Holy Scripture: always speak the truth—and back it up with your life. Say *yes* or *no* and *mean it*—without equivocation. This is the only way that dependable human relations can be preserved, and this is the only way that a man can be rightly related to God. When a man is confronted with the question of whether he will loyally support the constitution of the nation, he ought to say clearly *yes* or *no* and be ready to back it up with his life. To haggle over the technicality of whether an oath is required, or whether a solemn affirmation will do, or to refuse to take it in order to leave one an "out," is to fall into the same legalistic casuistry which Jesus so thoroughly condemned in the Pharisees. An honest man is always willing to declare himself, to say *yes* or *no*—and when he says it, he *means* it. This is the principle which echoes like a trumpet call down all the tortured centuries of man's deception and hypocrisy—speak the truth, simply and plainly, and do not compromise it by any kind of rationalization.

Discovering the Principle

There are several important steps which must be taken in order to discover the principle which underlies the biblical injunctions:

1. The first step is always the recovery of the historical circumstances which bear upon the scriptural teaching. This means, again, that all the archaeological evidence available must be evaluated. In the example of Corinth, above, it is the work of the archaeologist which revealed the temple of Aphrodite and its cult. Only by their recovery of this pagan temple and its practices was it possible to understand fully the situation with which Paul was dealing.

2. The second step is the attempt to state the same teaching in more general terms, without using the specific instance in the passage at hand. Take the case of the women in Corinth. The true question is whether there is something inherently wrong with a woman's speaking in public, or whether there is something in the situation at Corinth which makes it unwise for a Christian woman to speak out in public assembly. When examined in this way, it is clear, from the historical situation in Corinth, that the underlying issue is the danger of being mistaken for one of the pagan priestesses. After all, the women members of the church in Corinth were also females in a religious cult. They had to make a clear distinction between themselves and the women of the pagan cult. The more general purpose then could be stated in terms such as this: everywhere, and at all times, *all* Christians

should so conduct themselves that they will not be confused with those of evil purpose or bring reproach upon the Lord they serve.

3. The third step is the testing of the general statement against the background of other scriptural teaching. In the case of the women in Corinth, it would be of paramount importance to test the statement by the other statements of Paul, himself, on the same general subject. This same biblical writer, writing under the inspiration of the Holy Spirit, says that in Christ both male and female have exactly the same status (Gal. 3:28). If this passage in Corinthians is to be interpreted in such a way as to make the women "second-class Christians," not having the same privileges and responsibilities as the men, then it would be brought into direct contradiction with a fundamental teaching of Paul.

Also, it is important to test the statement against the wider background of other scriptural teachings. Does it fit with Jesus' attitude and teaching about women? Does it violate the basic biblical teaching of the equality of all people before God? Such a testing of any biblical teaching is essential to a proper interpretation of any particular passage.

4. The final step is the application of the principle to the life situation today. This cannot be done by a simple equation of circumstances in the first century with those in the twentieth. Usually these cannot be equated. The problem is more complex and more challenging. Having discovered what the biblical writer intended to accomplish by his words in the lives of his readers, it is necessary for us to try to accomplish this same purpose in the lives of our hearers. The principle must always be stated in terms which correspond to the *purpose* of the biblical writer, and the application of that principle to a life situation today must accomplish that *same pur-*

pose. If this identity of purpose is not preserved, the whole method which we have called "applying the principle" will be invalidated.

The Appropriate Use of This Method

In all of the examples given in the earlier chapters, it was clear that each type of biblical literature lends itself to one particular method of interpretation more than any other. The clearly defined patterns of the Psalms, the poetic sections of the prophets, or the many hymns and hymn fragments in Old and New Testament are most adaptable to a "pattern interpretation." The narrative sections, the vivid description of events, or the great stories of biblical heroes are most adaptable to the "you are there" approach. When these events are really made to live in vibrant language, the hearer can live through the event in his own mind.

In the same way, this method of "applying the principle" is most appropriate for certain types of Scripture passages. The passages which almost demand this type of interpretation, and can never be fully understood without it, are those which could be called moral teaching, or ethical exhortation. The ethical exhortations of the prophets were addressed to particular problems in ancient Israel, and they are almost never stated in the abstract language of a textbook of ethics. Some of the problems they faced are remarkably similar to some of the problems we face; and, in those cases, their words can be applied directly with a minimum of interpretation. But many of their teachings have no direct parallel to our day, and these must be carefully examined to find the underlying principle. Even those which seem to be a direct parallel can be very tricky. Sometimes, even when the parallel seems to be very close, there may be a world of difference.

The only safe guide in this instance is a thorough understanding of the historical situation.

All of the Epistles of the New Testament are filled with ethical teachings. All of the teaching sections in the Gospels are filled with the ethical exhortations of Jesus, and almost all of these require the method of interpretation outlined in this chapter. As in the case of the other methods of interpretation, this method can also be applied in conjunction with the others. There is an overlapping of various types of literature in the Bible, and there are values to be found in the application of various methods of interpretation to the same passages.

Perhaps no portion of the Bible is more amenable to this method of interpretation than the letters of Paul. In most of them there is a clearly defined ethical section, containing explicit guidance for the Christian life. Because Paul was writing to churches in different places, with many different backgrounds and problems, his letters are extremely relevant for our churches today. In a typical missionary situation where the churches are young and inexperienced, or threatened by legalism within and paganism without, the writings of Paul are even more explicit in their bearing upon the situation.

Because of this characteristic of the letters of Paul, one of them has been chosen to illustrate this method. In 1 Corinthians Paul was dealing with a series of problems which had arisen in the church at Corinth. He had received word of divisions in the church, of scandalous immorality openly condoned, of abuses of the Lord's Supper, of a confusion of tongue-speaking in the public worship, and many other problems. In addition, he had received a letter from them in which they asked him specific questions about the Christian life and conduct (v. 1).

Paul addressed himself pointedly to these problems, and he gave specific instructions and guidance in dealing with them. Because we now have a very full historical account of the situation in Corinth, we are able to "get inside" of these problems and find the principle which applies to our problems today. The following example will actually give a *series* of illustrations of the method of discovering and applying the principles, which Paul laid down, to our life situation today.

II. Example: "Guidelines for Christian Living"

There is a feeling abroad today that the old standards of moral conduct are completely irrelevant. They have "got to go"! They have been held up to ridicule and caricature until many modern young people simply dismiss with contempt anyone who refers to them. The standard of conduct becomes "what I want to do" or "anything that is *meaningful* to me."

Such a naive subjectivism is irrational in its very essence and terribly discredited by the record of human history. It seems almost incredible that intelligent people could fall victim to it. No sane man would take seriously a scientist who treated the laws of nature with contempt. If he tried to apply the law of gravity, or the principle of hydraulics, or the chemical function of a drug simply in the way he felt about it, rather than according to the clearly defined laws of nature, he could destroy everything he touched. Such a man in the field of airplane design, or automobile manufacture, or on the staff of a hospital, could kill more people than an army. If he could not be brought to his senses, he would have to be placed under restraint or committed to a mental institution.

Yet, in a painfully close analogy, there are "moral experts" by the dozens who are treating the moral laws of the universe with contempt. It may be that they do not believe there are any moral laws. In that case they are like the "mad scientist" who does not believe in natural laws. Moral laws are discovered and verified in a manner that is very similar to that used with natural laws: by careful observation and testing, by evaluating the rational coherence of each with that of others and with the whole of nature. The consequences of certain kinds of moral behavior have been observed in individuals and nations for as long as man has been upon this planet. Moral standards have been tested and tried for centuries, and the laboratory of human experience is replete with evidence for the dependability of many widely accepted moral principles.

For the Christian, the verification of certain moral principles by the prophets of the Old Testament, and especially the fulfilment of these principles in the supreme life of Jesus Christ, is sufficient authority for proclaiming eternal moral principles which can never be shaken! In a time of moral relativism, when people are honestly confused about what is right and what is wrong, this note of moral certainty needs to be sounded. It is grounded in the moral God of the universe, and it is expressed in the deeds and words of the prophets and apostles who have proclaimed the divine truth through the Holy Scriptures.

Paul the apostle is one man who was not afraid to say plainly what he believed and why he believed it. On more than one occasion he spelled out carefully the way in which he discovered a fundamental moral principle and how he intended to apply it to a specific situation. This is especially true in 1 Corinthians, a veritable textbook of moral principles. Let us follow the guidelines which Paul laid down for Christian ethical conduct.

Merely Lawful or Actually Helpful?

In 1 Corinthians 6:12, Paul lays down a principle which is
fundamental to all ethical conduct. In fact, it is fundamental
to life itself—"All things are lawful for me, but not all things
are helpful." The clause "all things are lawful to me" seems
to be a direct quotation from a letter the Corinthians had
written to Paul. Some of them were arguing that anything is
lawful—that is, that any kind of conduct is permitted. "Anything goes" is the modern equivalent. They were arguing this
way because they claimed that by grace they were free from
the legalistic demands of the Mosaic code. They had a measure of truth, but they were carrying it to a point where it
contradicted the truth of God.

"Yes," Paul replies, "everything is lawful"— and then he
goes on to explain what he means by "everything" and "lawful." He means that everything which God has made is good,
but it must be *used in a good and helpful way!* Paul knows
that everything which God created is good: our bodies, all of
the functions of our bodies, every plant that grows, everything in the whole creation. When God had finished it all, he
said, "It is good!"

The problem, then, is not that something in nature is bad,
but that man uses something in nature in a bad way. There
are some people that look upon the human body, especially
the sexual organs, as nasty or evil. There is no doubt that
human beings have often used their bodies in terribly evil
ways. But to condemn the body, or to condemn the sexual
function, is to blaspheme the Holy God! Who made our
bodies? Who made us male and female? Who designed our
bodily functions? From the Bible and from Christian experience, the answer comes back loud and clear: God made us—

God created our bodies—God is the author of our lives. To treat God's creation with contempt is to treat God with contempt. It is the act of a moral reprobate. Responsible moral action requires that we use the natural order in the way which the Creator intended. This intention of the Creator is expressed in the way that he has made all things, and in the revealed truth which he has communicated through his prophets and apostles across the ages.

In the midsummer, there are few delights to compare with tantalizingly fresh "corn on the cob." Taken from the field when the tender little grains have just formed, dropped ever so briefly into a pan of boiling water, buttered and peppered and salted from one end to the other—it is pure ambrosia, food for the gods! Like so many of the marvels of God's creation, it is an expression of his gracious bounty and provision for his children.

Yet, men can take this delightful and wholesome food and turn it into something which is wicked in its uses. They can throw this corn into a mash, distil the fermenting solution, bottle it and sell it as a drug which enslaves and kills more people than all other drugs put together! People try to defend this action by saying, "It is lawful" or "If they would just use it right we would not have all this trouble from liquor." All these flimsy ways of trying to excuse a vicious evil will break up on the one principle which Paul lays down at the very foundation of our lives: "Is it helpful?" Even if you argue that a thing may be all right, or that "it won't hurt too much," or "everybody is doing it," you are still dodging the inescapable principle: anything we *make,* anything we *use,* anything we *do,* anything we *say*—must be *helpful.* Otherwise, it falls below God's ethical standard. A man who engages in that which is destructive, rather than helpful, is doing the work of the devil—for that is his name, *Apollyon,* the Destroyer!

Now there is a principle to live by—concentrate on that which is helpful in everything you do—it is the fundamental moral law of the universe, because it is the will of God for the creature he made in his own image. Name anything you want to name—games, movies, current fads, personal relationships, jobs, church programs—everyone has to be measured by this same principle. Is it helpful and constructive, or is it harmful and destructive? Does it carry out the purpose of God as revealed in nature and in his Holy Word, or does it contradict it? In most cases, the answer is so plain that a "wayfaring man though a fool" cannot miss it!

Liberating or Enslaving?

In the latter part of 1 Corinthians 6:12, Paul carries his point further, laying down another principle. It grows out of the basic one (do only that which is *helpful*), but it takes a specific form. Repeating the argument used by the Corinthians in their letter (all things are lawful), Paul again says, "Yes," and then qualifies it in a very important way—"but I will not be enslaved by anything." Anything which enslaves the body, mind, or spirit, is wrong. We belong to the Creator, and the Christian belongs to Christ—body and soul. Everything within our whole being is committed to his lordship. "You are not your own; you were bought with a price. So glorify God in your body" (vv. 19,20, RSV).

One of the most shattering experiences one can ever have is to visit a narcotics hospital. Rooms barred like prison cells contain mainly young people, pitifully "hooked" on drugs. Sometimes heavy mittens are drawn over their hands to keep them from clawing their faces—or padding lines the walls and bars to reduce the danger of injury. No wonder parents became so incensed at the drug traffic and the preying upon schoolchildren that they stormed Washington with demands for heavy penalties upon all the drug pushers and handlers.

Yet, there is a strange inconsistency here. A few hundred thousand, at most, are addicted to the heroin derivatives and the other drugs which enslave the mind and body. But between five and eight *million* Americans are horribly addicted to alcohol! There is more death on the highways, more crime and violence, more broken homes and hearts because of alcohol than all other drugs put together! How can people cry out even for the death penalty for those who peddle the other drugs, and in the same breath legalize and justify the one which is actually doing the greatest damage of all? The shocking inconsistency of this is enough to make you wonder about the capacity of the human mind to rationalize evil.

Any habit which enslaves the body, mind, or spirit—whether it is drinking, smoking, "shooting dope," or vicious gossiping—is wrong! It is wrong because we belong to our Lord, and we must keep ourselves free to serve him.

Purifying or Defiling?

In 1 Corinthians 6:19, Paul uses a graphic figure which portrays another principle: "Do you not know that your body is a temple of the Holy Spirit within you, which you have from God?"

The Old Testament picture of holiness is the Temple, with its Holy Place and holy of holies, and an elaborate ritual to insure absolute purity of the priest and the sacred objects. Paul, with his clear understanding of the work of Christ—of the Temple veil rent in twain at the death of Jesus and his indwelling of the Christian believer—sees that the new temple

is the body of the Christian. "Christ liveth in me" (Gal.
2:20), and this dwelling place of Christ, through the Holy
Spirit must be kept clean and pure.

Here is the principle: anything which defiles the body,
mind, or spirit is wrong—because this is the dwelling place of
the Holy Spirit. He dwells not in stones, or trees, or brick
buildings, but in the living body of the Christian believer.
Any book or movie which fills the mind with impurity—any
habit or amusement which corrupts or harms the body—any
ugly attitude or action which mars the spirit—is wrong! It is
wrong because it is destroying the temple in which God
dwells. We cannot argue that it is our life, and we can do
what we please; it is *his* life, and we must do what the Lord
pleases.

Bridge or Stumbling Block?

In 1 Corinthians 8, Paul takes up the thorny issue of "food
offered to idols." Virtually all the meat sold in the Roman
meat markets had been sacrificed in some pagan temple. For
the "stronger" Christian, this might create no problem at all,
because he knew that there was nothing to this idol worship
anyway. But, in this chapter, Paul introduces another principle which goes far beyond the question of meat sacrificed to
idols. He can acknowledge the argument that food, in itself,
is morally neutral—it does not commend us to God. However,
the effect of our action upon a weaker brother is a serious
matter, and Paul spells it out clearly: "Only take care lest this
liberty of yours somehow become a stumbling block to the
weak. For if any one sees you, a man of knowledge, at table
in an idol's temple, might he not be encouraged, if his con-
science is weak, to eat food offered to idols?" (vv. 9-10).

It is our responsibility to build bridges for the younger and weaker Christian and not to put stumbling blocks in his way. Paul condemns this callous disregard for the welfare of the weaker one: "And so by your knowledge this weak man is destroyed, the brother for whom Christ died" (v. 11). He even adds that by sinning against a weaker brother in this way we are sinning against Christ (v. 12)!

Thus, another principle shines clearly through the issue Paul is facing: we must ask not only, "Does it hurt me?" but we must add: "Does it cause someone else to stumble?" There are enough stumbling blocks in the way for the new Christians and the younger people. We need to help them get over the dangerous places—not add to their problems.

Any habit—any amusement—any practice—in the life of the Christian must pass this influence test. Not only must it be clear of the charge of enslaving or defiling the Christian, but it must not cause another to be hurt by the example.

Constructive or Destructive?

Paul continues his application of basic principles to the specific problems in Corinth by dealing with the abuses of the Lord's Supper, support for those who preach the gospel, and further aspects of the problem of meat sacrificed to idols. In 1 Corinthians 10:23, he propounds a principle which is universal in its scope. It has been in the background of his advice and instructions on many subjects, but he makes it explicit at this point:

"All things are lawful," as the Corinthians have said to Paul in their letter, "but not all things are helpful. All things are lawful, but not all things build up." There are the key words—"build up"!

With a clear theological basis which goes all the way back to the doctrine of creation, Paul declares that a thing must have a constructive effect in order to be right. It must be more than merely *lawful,* it must "build up" the body, mind, or spirit. If the whole person is not helped by it, Paul is convinced that it is wrong.

When people argue that they can engage in some questionable activity, because it "won't hurt too much," they are actually arguing in an irrational way. One might whack himself on the head with a hammer and insist that he can do this without hurting himself too much, but such a person would be considered insane and placed under restraint for his own protection. Millions of people are engaging in habits, "amusements," and patterns of conduct which tear down the health of the body, actually hurt the mind and its awesome capacities, or corrupt the spirit which gives ultimate meaning to life. When these people argue that they can do these things without hurting themselves too much, they are arguing in such an irrational way that their judgment is called into question.

This glaring inconsistency is pointed out by Paul as he enunciates the principle: anything we do must serve a constructive purpose—if it is destructive of body, mind, or spirit, it is wrong in the sight of God.

Many young people want to know if they can read a certain off-color book, or see a certain salacious movie, or engage in a particular questionable conduct without its "hurting them too much." Such a question is exactly backwards! We ought to ask, "What is the *best* book I can read?" or "What is the best movie I can see?" We must do the things which will build up our minds, our spirits, and our bodies—not the things which will fill them with filth and destruction. This principle can be applied to almost any question of conduct, and it would save earnest Christians from many a pitfall. The

Creator, in his loving action, was constructive in everything he made; only those who use their lives for constructive purposes are in his service. Those who hurt, and tear down, and destroy are in league with the Evil One—the Destroyer. Destruction is his business, and he is able to enlist many thoughtless accomplices!

Human Selfishness or God's Glory?

We may conclude this study of the ethical principles which Paul expressed in 1 Corinthians by looking at the one which is the most comprehensive of all. It actually includes all the others, and it gives coherence to the entire ethical approach which Paul used.

In a verse which Paul apparently intended as a summary of his ethical instruction, this key insight is found: "So, whether you eat or drink, or whatever you do, do all to the glory of God" (10:31). This is certainly an all-inclusive principle. "Whatever you do" includes everything, and everything is measured by one standard: does it glorify God?

Most people today have a strange idea about the "glory of God." It sounds as if it could include only worship in the church, singing in the choir, or going to Sunday School classes. But, throughout the Bible, the phrase "glorifying God" has a very specific meaning. The "glory of God" is his innermost being, or nature. When he discloses his glory, whether in word or event, he is making known his innermost being and sharing his holy love with men. Therefore, when we do something to the glory of God, we are showing forth in our lives and actions the very nature of the living God. If we minister to the suffering of the downtrodden, we are showing the compassionate love of God through our deeds. If we plunge into the scientific quest for the meaning and rela-

tionships of the natural order, we are showing forth the infinite handiwork of the Creator. If we share in a sports contest
with zest and fairplay, we are showing forth the joy and the
striving which God had planted in all of his creatures.

Let this supreme principle be our guideline in all things:
may we so conduct ourselves that in everything we do the
very nature of the loving Father shines through! Can any
principle ever surpass this?

III. Analysis

The relevance of this method of interpretation is apparent
at every step in the example just given. Application of the
principles to current ethical issues could be multiplied end-
lessly. There is sometimes room for debate about the application to particular issues; but, if the principle is clearly per-
ceived and accurately stated, the application is usually
obvious.

Words of Caution

Because the Bible is so often misused as a club over people's heads, a few words of warning might be appropriate:

1. Always make a specific application of the principle to a
contemporary issue. Even if it is highly debatable, and there
are differences of opinion on it, the principle must be fo-
cused on a particular issue in order for it to be relevant and
meaningful.

2. Try to make the principle stand out so clearly that the
hearer cannot reject the principle, even though he may haggle
over your particular application. Confront him with a situation in which he must make his own application, and let him
wrestle with it until the principle has laid hold of him.

3. Stick to the issues which are rooted in the deepest theological foundations. It is pointless and harmful to haggle

about matters of personal preference, or custom, or traditional behavior, when they have no real bearing upon the deepest purpose of God in his creation. Sometimes mothers have engaged in violent arguments over a daughter's hair style, or a son's sideburns, while a deeper issue of moral conduct was overlooked. Save your ammunition for the issues that really count—and have a reason for what you say. It must be rooted in the very nature of God, and man as God has created him, or it will not stand the test!

4. Finally, remember that these principles, or moral laws, can be validated by the careful observation of human life and welfare. Even if some people reject the authority of the Bible, or try to dismiss the reality of God, they cannot deny the fact of human life. By a method that is as valid as that of the natural sciences, it can be shown that moral laws affect and control human welfare. Do not shrink from the man who ridicules God or the Bible. If he can think at all, he will be compelled to face the question of moral principles. For the believer, the will of God as expressed in the Scriptures will be the supreme authority.

The Value of This Approach

An interpreter must pay the price of long and intensive study of the historical backgrounds of the Scripture passages, if he is to use this method effectively. But the rewards surpass any evaluation. This world is literally desperate for guidance in the area of moral and ethical standards. There is no other way to bring the message of the Bible to bear with such force upon the lives of men today.

No matter how vital the message may have been in the day of Amos, or of Paul, it must be made to live in the hearts of men today—or it will have no effect. The challenge is enormous, and the dividends reach to all eternity.

5

Finding the Key

Keys are made to unlock things. It might seem that this is only half the truth. Are they not made to *lock* as well as *un*lock things? Indeed, some locks require a key for locking as well as unlocking, although many do not. A lock itself is designed to secure something against general access. It is intended to limit access to the one who has the key!

As everyone knows, keys can be lost. Nothing is more exasperating than to find that the keys have been misplaced —or, most frustrating of all, locked up in the very car, or trunk, or house one is trying to open. In this situation, the lock is preventing access to the key which was designed to open it!

There is a remarkable literary parallel to this common experience with keys. Many types of literature are deliberately designed to "lock up" the meaning from all who do not have, or cannot find, the key. And, in closest parallel, it may be necessary to "break in" and get the key, in order to have easy access thereafter. In either case, possession of the key is essential for smooth operation of the lock.

The Key to the Parables

According to Mark's Gospel, Jesus deliberately used parables to conceal his message from those who did not have the "key" and to open it for those who had the "key": "And he said unto them, Unto you it is given to know the mystery of the kingdom of God: but unto them that are without, all these things are done in parables: that seeing they may see, and not perceive; and hearing they may hear, and not understand" (Mark 4:11-12, KJV).

Apparently the "key," in this case, was the attitude of the hearer. If the hearer had an attitude of openness and trust in Jesus, this was the key which unlocked the meaning of the parables. Only from a position of humility and trust could the right perspective be obtained for seeing and understanding the message of Christ. If one reacted to Jesus with resentment and hostility, like the Pharisees, he was blinded to the truth which was concealed in the very simple language of his parables.

Unlocking the Meaning

In the parables, and in many other portions of the Scriptures, the meaning is hidden from those who do not have this attitude of trust and expectancy. This is why so many people do not find the Bible interesting or meaningful for their lives. It is faith which unlocks the treasures of the Scriptures; and faith, in turn, is strengthened by the truth unfolded through the Word of God.

In reading the parables, or the accounts of the miracles of Jesus, or a great event in the history of Israel, it often happens that the key idea is spelled out in specific words. That is, the element which appeals to faith is expressly stated in pointed language. The reason for this is that the Scriptures were written for a faith response! They were not written simply to record some ancient history, or to aid in spiritual meditation, or to start a new religion. They were written in order that men might *believe:* "But these are written, that you may believe that Jesus is the Christ, the Son of God, and that believing you may have life in his name" (John 20:31).

"Meaning for faith"—this is the key to the Bible. In almost every passage of Scripture it is possible to find the key idea which lays claim on our faith. It is this which transcends the centuries in between and makes the ancient words significant for our life today. The relevance of the Bible is entirely dependent upon this all-important aspect of interpretation. Too many commentaries and too many Bible teachers have been content to report what Jeremiah said to Judah or what Paul said to the Corinthians. Even a detailed and scientific study of the ancient language and history is not enough. If we know everything that a passage of Scripture meant in its original setting, we are only halfway to our goal. We must ask what it means for faith today! We must ask how it affects what we believe and the way we live. This is the "meaning for faith" which must be found if the interpreter is to fulfil his purpose.

So What?

Too often the biblical interpreter leaves his hearers with an unspoken question forming in their minds. "Yes, the Israelites had a big Temple, and they offered sacrifices, but what does that have to do with us?" Paul was obviously concerned about "meat sacrificed to idols," but what on earth does that mean for believers today? Although this question could be asked in an arrogant and contemptuous way, it is actually the most important question of all. The "so what?" is the reason the Scriptures were written in the first place. The "so what?" is the reason we search the Scriptures today. The interpreter who does not ask and attempt to answer this question is forfeiting his calling.

I. Steps in Finding the Key

There are some simple steps which should be taken in the effort to find the key to each biblical passage:

1. Read and reread the passage in order to discover *why* the particular Scripture was written in the first place. What was the original writer, the prophet or apostle, trying to accomplish in his hearers? Often it is necessary to read the wider context, to know the historical situation, and, especially, to know the exact group to which he was speaking.

This purpose which the author had in mind is the clue to everything else. It accounts for the words he uses, the particular style he employs, and for every detail which is included or excluded from the scriptural record. No effort can be spared in the attempt to discover what the author was trying to accomplish with his words. This will open the first door of interpretation.

2. Try to discover why the community of Israel or the early church preserved this particular passage of Scripture. It is important to remember that all of the Scriptures were preserved by a community of faith. In the case of the Old Testament, it was the covenant people of Israel which recorded and preserved the words of the prophets. From the very dawn of their existence as the people of the covenant, Israel sang of the mighty deeds of Yahweh as he delivered them from Egyptian slavery. Around the campfires, in the family circle, and in the tabernacle, they celebrated the divine providence which guided them through every trial.

Why did they preserve certain narratives, poems, or psalms, and not others? The answer to this question will go a long way toward explaining the meaning which the particular Scripture had for their community of faith. It spoke to some need in their life, and it laid a claim upon their hearts and minds as the Word of God for them. Otherwise, it would never have been recorded and preserved as a part of the sacred writings.

3. By a careful study of key words in the passage, try to discover how Israel or the early church *used* a particular Scripture. We now know that virtually everything in the Bible was used in the worship of Israel, in the preaching of early Christian evangelists, or in the teaching of new converts to the faith. The most positive results of decades of work by scholars who study the sources and the literary form of the Scriptures have taken place in this area.

Many people fear the work of the "form critic" as he seeks to discover how a Scripture was preserved orally, and then written, and how it was used in the life of the church or in the covenant community of Israel. They think this detracts from the direct inspiration of the Scriptures. The truth is that it throws more light on how the Lord worked to accomplish the miracle of his written Word. He worked in the prophet or apostle who wrote it, in the hearts of the believers who received and preserved it, and he works in our lives today as we seek to interpret it. Anyone who has a doctrine of inspiration which leaves out any of these steps has an incomplete and very inadequate doctrine.

By a study of the history of the spread of Christianity into the Gentile world, it is possible to see how some of the parables of Jesus, or some of the explanations of Jewish customs in the Gospels, were used. Sometimes they had a very special meaning when they were addressed to a Gentile audience. When we see how they took the words of Jesus, spoken in Palestine to a Jewish audience, and applied them to a Gentile situation in Rome or Ephesus, it gives us guidance on how to apply them to our situation today.

4. By a process of elimination, we have to look for the key which unlocks all the locks—the master key. In many of the parables, it is possible to find *several key ideas*. In the parable of the good Samaritan, for example, one could find a clue to the meaning by concentrating upon:

(1) the preoccupation of the priest with religious duties, to the exclusion of human need;

(2) the tendency of the Levite, a "staff member" of the Temple, to follow the example of the priest;

(3) the hatred between the Jewish and Samaritan people;

(4) the startling fact that a Samaritan would even bother to help a Jew;

(5) the unselfish compassion which the Samaritan had for a man in distress—even a Jewish man;

(6) the value of *action* over merely feeling compassion for one in need;

(7) the willingness to see a problem through to the end, as shown by the Samaritan's leaving money and promising to pay any further bill upon his return.

Doubtless, all of these ideas have some validity. Yet, they do not stand on equal footing, because all other ideas must depend at last upon the main one—the one which is the reason for the parable in the first place. Many preachers and teachers, in the effort to wring everything possible out of a Scripture, will "sermonize" upon it to the very limits of their imagination. For example, from the parable of the good Samaritan, people have been warned of the dangers of traveling alone, of taking the *downward* road (from Jerusalem *down* to Jericho), of putting their trust in the clergy (priests and Levites), or of the medicinal values of oil and wine (which were poured on the poor man's wounds). Some have even waxed eloquent upon the lowly beast which bore the wounded man, a fitting symbol of the church which bears the broken lives upon her back. Because the beast stands on four legs, some interpreters have even ventured to name the four pillars of the church—faith, hope, love, and a fourth leg which limps between virtue, knowledge, and temperance.

Surely it is obvious to anyone that there is no limit to such an exercise except the ingenuity of the "interpreter." It would be laughable if it were not so dangerous. These are ideas which the interpreter already had, however good or bad they may be, and he simply looks for something to "hang" them on in the biblical text. They are not derived from the text; they are read *into* the text.

5. A crucial step in the process of "finding the key" comes at this point. When a careful study of the text reveals one or more ideas which clearly emerge from the text itself, the interpreter is faced with this question: which one is fundamental to all the others. Which one actually accounts for and supports the others in a way which makes it the basic idea in the passage.

It is essential that the interpreter find this basic clue, because it will be his guide in the use which he makes of the Scripture in preaching or teaching today. This basic clue will also be the standard by which all other ideas are evaluated. Any idea which does not grow out of this basic one is suspect. However valid it may be in itself, it cannot be a part of the biblical meaning unless it grows out of the key idea in the text.

In the case of the parable of the good Samaritan, Jesus was answering the question, "Who is my neighbor?" by showing what it meant to *be a neighbor*—by an act of love and compassion to a man in dire distress, the Samaritan *was a neigh-*

bor to a man who was anything but a "neighbor" in the usual
definition of the term. He was saying that we must act in love
and mercy to meet human need even when the person does
not live near us, or when he belongs to another race, and
when everybody else (even the church) is passing him by.
Every other valid idea which is drawn from the parable must
be derived from this basic purpose of the parable. *This is the
key!* As the key it will unlock other insights in the parable
and throw light upon the teaching of Jesus in other situations. Also, this key is the controlling factor in applying the
teaching of the parable (or any other passage of Scripture) to
our life situation today.

6. The last step in this process is the utilization of the key.
The key idea opens up the meaning of a passage for the
Christian faith and life today. Any application of the message
of a scriptural text to a contemporary problem or situation
must be tested by this "key" to the meaning. In the case of
the parable of the good Samaritan, the application of this
text to our concern for men of other races is valid because
the fundamental key to the parable is concern for others in
need, even when they do not belong to our particular group.
The application of the text to our concern for all human
suffering and need is also valid, because this is an expression
of the fundamental clue to the parable. Even the warning to
the religious institution (the church) that she had better be
more concerned about human need than about her religious
rituals is also expressly spelled out by Jesus in his designation
of the priest and the Levite who hurried on about their business, ignoring the suffering man.

However, the spiritualizing of the text to warn against taking the "downward way," or to draw parallels to church-staff
relationships (priest and Levite), is to depart entirely from

the key idea of the parable. This becomes a distortion and misuse of Scripture. However true a moralistic injunction may be, it is wrong to base it upon a Scripture which does not teach it. The key idea must control the interpretation of a passage of Scripture and the application of it to our life situation today.

Determining the Use of This Method

As in every other type of Scripture interpretation, this method of "finding the key" is applicable to certain types of Scripture passages more than others. It is ideal for the parables of Jesus. In fact, even in conjunction with other methods, it is almost indispensable to the interpretation of the parables. There is literally no way to unlock the full meaning of a parable without this key.

However, this method is also valuable in testing and supporting other forms of interpretation. For example, in the story of the sacrifice of Isaac, developed in chapter 1 of this book by the method of dramatic involvement in the event, this method of the "key" would be a wonderful aid in discovering the meaning of the narrative. The key idea is spelled out very clearly in the words of Abraham: "My son, God will provide himself a lamb for a burnt offering" (Gen. 22:8). We know this is the key because Abraham called this mountain by the name *"Jehovah-jireh," the Lord will provide* (v. 14). Any interpretation or application of this narrative for our spiritual edification today must grow out of this basic key. It must show that in response to a man's faith God will provide to the uttermost for his deepest need. Such a use of the "key" will protect the interpreter from some wild application of the passage in a way which contradicts its fundamental meaning.

This method is also especially applicable to those narratives in the Gospels (or elsewhere) which end with a pointed summary statement. For example, when Jesus and his disciples went through the grainfields on the sabbath and plucked the grain, Jesus replied to the outraged Pharisees with this pronouncement: "The sabbath was made for man, and not man for the sabbath: therefore the Son of man is Lord also of the sabbath" (Mark 2:27-28). Clearly, this is the key to the whole passage. This tells us why the episode was remembered and recorded in the first place. It also shows us that the early Christians were using this to demonstrate the superiority of the lordship of Jesus Christ to any sabbath regulation invoked by legalistic Judaizers.

The "key" method is also very valuable in studying the individual oracles of the great prophets of Israel, or the entire books of the shorter or "minor" prophets. In many cases, the key idea becomes the stack pole around which the entire message of the prophet can be arranged: for Hosea, the steadfast love of God (*chesed*) is clearly the key to the whole book. Without the discovery of this key, almost nothing else in the book could be understood. The application of Hosea's message at any point must be governed by this fundamental theme of the prophet: God's steadfast love continues to lay its claim upon the people of Israel, no matter how many times they have "played the harlot" and chased after other gods!

In the case of Amos, the obvious key is the thundering "righteousness of God," which will shatter sinful Israel and the nations, but which is also her only hope for redemption. In these examples, the central key for an entire book is of paramount importance in opening up the meaning of each paragraph or small unit of the book.

Just as the wider context must always be kept in mind in interpreting any unit of Scripture, so the key idea must be the controlling factor in the interpretation of any verse or paragraph within the entire book. If the interpreter comes out with an isolated interpretation which conflicts with the basic idea of the book, something is obviously wrong. Usually it means that the interpretation is wrong. Sometimes biblical scholars find in this circumstance compelling evidence for multiple sources or conflation of separate strands of tradition in a particular book or document.

Thus, there is a wide use for this method of interpretation. It is the supreme method for most parables and for those narratives which contain a key "pronouncement" near the end. It is also an important adjunct to other methods in interpreting almost all other Scriptures. It has a special wider application to the shorter epistles of the New Testament and to the minor prophets, because these briefer writings tend to cluster around a central key. No interpreter can safely ignore this important search for the "key." Without that key, much of the biblical message will never be unlocked.

II. Example: The Pharisee and the Tax Collector

Have you ever wished that you might have been down beside the Sea of Galilee one day, to hear Jesus preach? Would you like to have been among that throng which sat down upon the beach while Jesus taught from the boat?

We need not grieve about our loss in being born nearly 2,000 years too late. As a matter of fact, we probably have an even better opportunity to hear and understand the message of Jesus than they did! Through inspired writers, the message of Jesus was recorded for us to hear. Through devout and dedicated translators, the words are brought into our own language. Against the background of long centuries of interpretation and discovery, the words of Jesus shine like luminous stars to guide us on the way. And, within our hearts at this moment, the Holy Spirit lives to interpret the words and illuminate our minds. We *can* hear Jesus preach again, and we can hear his words with compelling power! Will you listen as we hear again the wonderful words of a little "sermon" Jesus preached—

"Two men went up into the temple to pray, one a Pharisee and the other a tax collector. The Pharisee stood and prayed thus with himself, 'God, I thank thee that I am not like other men, extortioners, unjust, adulterers, or even like this tax collector. I fast twice a week, I give tithes of all that I get.' But the tax collector, standing far off, would not even lift up his eyes to heaven, but beat his breast, saying, 'God, be merciful to me a sinner!' I tell you, this man went down to his house justified rather than the other; for every one who exalts himself will be humbled, but he who humbles himself will be exalted" (Luke 18:10-14).

Then Jesus blessed the little children, illustrating by the humility of a child the central point of his message. He answered the question of the rich young ruler about eternal life, and then he went on his way on the last journey to Jerusalem —where he *humbled himself* and became obedient unto death.

No glimpse of the life and Word of Jesus is more revealing than this brief insight into his ministry and this unforgettable vignette of the two men in the Temple. Yet, its meaning is so easy to miss! Without the key which unlocks this marvelous story, the whole message can be lost.

Because Jesus often condemned the hypocrisy of the Pharisees, it is quite natural to read this story as another condemnation of their casuistry and hyperlegalism. Were they not all hypocrites? Who did this Pharisee think he was to tell God how good he was, when, all the time, he was probably as two-faced a hypocrite as the rest of them?

But, to read the parable in this typical way is to miss

several important clues. Luke is careful to tell us that Jesus addressed this parable to some "who trusted in themselves that they were righteous" (Luke 18:9). Now this means that the man he describes must really exemplify human righteousness, or the whole point is missed. If the Pharisee were simply a hypocrite, and not a truly devout and righteous man, then the entire message Jesus is seeking to communicate would be invalidated.

Also, it is clear throughout the parable that Jesus is describing a truly religious man—a devout and faithful follower of the law of Moses. In the case of the tax collector, it is just as clear that Jesus is describing a man who can lay no claim to his own righteousness. He really is a guilty sinner. It is this contrast which clinches the point of the parable. As if this were not enough, Luke also reinforces this central purpose of the parable by including the account of the blessing of the little children immediately after. The lesson of humility before God, rather than self-righteous pride, is "driven home" by a sign as well as by his words.

With these clues it is impossible to miss the key to the message of Jesus. He is not condemning the hypocrisy of the Pharisees in this parable. And he is certainly not suggesting that it is better to be a flagrant sinner like the tax collector than to be a devout and upright man like the Pharisee. He is clearly saying that the devout Pharisee, with all his righteousness, can never be good enough to merit the approval of God. And the tax collector, with all his sin, is not beyond the grace of God. All men, however religious or however wicked, fall short of the divine standard; and their only approach to God is to cast themselves upon his mercy and grace! To trust in one's own righteousness is to bring spiritual catastrophe.

With this "key" let us open up the parable:

"Two men went up into the temple to pray . . ." From the

very beginning Jesus is stressing identity and contrast. Men are all actually on the same footing before God, even when some think they are so much better than others. In the parable *both* go up to the Temple, and both go up to *pray*. The fact that Jesus stresses this identity of purpose alerts us to the contrast he is about to project.

"One a Pharisee and the other a tax collector . . ." Jesus deliberately chose the most dramatic extremes. A Pharisee was the very acme of righteousness through the law. Some were very hypocritical—they are severely indicted by Jesus on more than one occasion. But many of them were the most devout and dedicated men which any religion has ever produced. The entire purpose of the parable depends upon this fact. Jesus chose a man who was a dedicated keeper of the law, a very paragon of moral righteousness, to depict the highest reaches of man's goodness before God.

On the other end of the scale, at the bottom of the moral ladder, was the tax collector. Because these men had sold themselves to the Roman oppressors, as collaborators and traitors, to wring the conqueror's tax from the victims of tyranny, they were understandably hated by the Jews. These were fellow-Jews, who profited by becoming tools in the hand of the enemy. Moreover, many of them were corrupt in other ways. They were considered to be moral reprobates, and it is likely that Jesus intended for us to understand that the tax collector was almost everything the Pharisee *was not*—extortioner, unjust, adulterer.

At any rate, the contrast is sharply and clearly drawn. The Pharisee was the highest expression of moral goodness; the tax collector was the embodiment of moral degradation. With this contrast, the stage is set: both men go up to the Temple, and both go to pray. But there the similarity ends—in their character and personal life they could not be more different!

"The Pharisee stood and prayed thus with himself . . ." With bold strokes and the fewest words Jesus sharpens the contrast. The Pharisee did not come to talk to God. He really came to preen himself. He is not interested in a deeper relationship with God. He is anxious to tell anyone who will listen, especially himself, how truly wonderful he is. It does not take a graduate psychologist to see through this. All this praise of himself covered a deep insecurity in this man. Deep down in his heart, he knew that all his moral attainments had never been able to remove a still deeper sense of guilt and spiritual inadequacy. He was talking loud to convince himself—and to keep his mind off this nagging doubt deep down in his soul.

And he said it—right out loud—"God, I thank thee that I am not like other men." We almost have to suppress a chuckle. Oh, the unmitigated arrogance of the man! Yet, with a moment's reflection, we may be more disturbed than amused. He simply said, right out loud, what most of us inwardly take for granted. Most of us think we are rather special. We think laws were mainly made for other people; and, in our case, can be adjusted a bit. We cry "foul" when we are the victims of the kind of gossip we "dish out" for others. We constantly think that we ought to be excused for the foibles and aberrations which we so soundly condemn in others. For shame! The Pharisee is more honest than we! He says openly what we try to conceal with hypocritical niceties.

Now, do not miss this—*he really was a good man.* On the authority of Jesus himself, we are viewing the portrait of a man who was the embodiment of moral excellence. You cannot fault him.

He was no *extortioner!* This word designated every kind of deception and chicanery which goes on in the name of "business." To take advantage of someone in a business deal—to put on the pressure and exact all that the traffic will bear—to victimize the unfortunate for personal gain—this is extortion. And it is the stock in trade for too many church members today! For the Jewish tax collector, it was a way of life. Give this Pharisee credit. He was straight and honest in all his dealings. You could trust your life to him.

He was not *unjust!* The little word "just" is one of the biggest words in the Bible. Its basic meaning is "straight" or "right." One who lived his life straight in line with the moral law of God was just or righteous. This the Pharisee could also say. Perhaps, like another devout man who came to Jesus, he could say, "All these laws I have kept from my youth up." Measured by the straightedge of the moral law, the Pharisee was a righteous man.

He was no *adulterer!* This is more than a lot of church members can say today. His children were not ashamed to call him "Father," and his wife could trust his faithfulness and steadfast love. He was the kind of man who commanded the confidence and respect of everyone—and the deep love and gratitude of his family.

Nor was this all! This man did not have to glory simply in what he was *not.* Look at what he did. "I fast twice a week . . ." Do you know what that means? The best Bible scholars we have are constantly searching into the background of the biblical words and practices. Apparently, this man belonged to a devout group which set aside two entire days each week for unbroken prayer and fasting. Before the sun came up over Mount Olivet, Mr. Pharisee could be seen wending his way up to the Temple—to lie on his face in prayer and fasting—from sunup until sundown, two days every week! There are church members today who are outraged if Sunday dinner is even a few minutes late. They wouldn't miss *one* meal for Jesus, much less spend two whole days of fasting. In devotion to God through the law of Moses, the Pharisee puts most Christians to shame!

"I give tithes of all that I get!" Note that—t-i-t-h-e-s— plural! He gave tithes, and tithes of tithes, and offerings! Again, the Bible students who have studied the practice of the Pharisees tell us that they regularly gave multiple tithes and offerings. Many of them faithfully gave up to half and more than half of their income to the service of the Lord. And these Pharisees were *laymen,* not priests who lived by the offerings of the Temple. They outdid the requirement of the law!

Now, brace yourself for the shocker! This *good* man—this moral, upright, devout, God-fearing man went down to his house *lost!* How can this be? If such a man as this is condemned, who then can be saved?

With a single sentence Jesus sketches in the picture of the other man who went up to the Temple to pray—that tax collector. Unworthy even to approach the altar of the Lord, he stood afar off. Overwhelmed with remorse for his sin, he beat his breast—a sign of grief and contrition. And he prayed a one-line prayer. Listen to that prayer! "God, be merciful to me a sinner!" He really was a sinner, and he knew his only hope was the grace of God. In deepest humility, he renounced all claim to his own righteousness and cast himself upon the mercy of God.

How the words of Jesus must have fallen like a thunderbolt upon his stunned hearers. "I tell you, *this man*—this sinful tax collector—went down to his house *justified* (made right with God) rather than the other." Is the whole world turned upside down? Is good bad and bad good? Is right wrong and wrong right? How can a good, moral man be lost and a bad man be saved?

In a ringing sentence which closes the parable, Jesus answers the question which is forming in everybody's mind: "For every one who exalts himself will be humbled, but he who humbles himself will be exalted." Shattering all human pride, rejecting all human philosophies, moral systems, and religions, Jesus makes it clear that there is only one way to come to God—in simple confession of sin and surrender to the grace of God.

"For by grace are ye saved through faith; and that not of yourselves: it is the gift of God: not of works, lest any man should boast" (Eph. 2:8-9, KJV). This is the heart of the gospel. So long as a man trusts his own righteousness, however noble, he cannot avail with God. When a man comes in humility and confession, however great his sin, he will be accepted by a gracious God.

This is the key which unlocks the whole message of Jesus. Did ever a sinner hear such a marvelous word as this?

III. Analysis of the Method

Most of the steps in the method of "finding the key" were illustrated in the example of the Pharisee and the tax collector. However, it may be helpful to call attention to some of these in the light of the particular example which has been put before us.

The search for the key idea was conducted in the full view of the listeners, or readers. This is important. They cannot be expected to accept the key idea upon the authority of the interpreter. They must be convinced of its validity by being drawn into the search for the key from the very first. This requires a look at the context of the Scripture passage and an overview of the entire passage before it is developed in detail.

Also, the key idea must be expressed in such a way that the element of surprise or anticipation is not entirely lost. The interpreter must still be able to unlock something with the key which he has found. If he discovers the key, and still cannot open up anything more, he has drawn a blank. There is little value in jangling keys which do not open any doors or treasure chests.

Showing How the Key Fits

Probably the most important factor in the development of the interpretation is the demonstration that the key fits every part of the scriptural text. In the example above, it was necessary to keep this key in mind as the two figures in the parable were introduced, and as each phrase or word unfolded in the heart of the text. The key opened up the sharp contrast between the Pharisee and the tax collector and highlighted the difference in their character. Most important, it prepared the hearer to feel, with great force, the difference in their attitudes. There was enough anticipation on the part of the listener that he could not miss the point when the text was opened up in its entirety. Each element in the description of the Pharisee and each word and action of the tax collector was opened up by the "key" of humility before God.

Evaluating the Method

The question which best evaluates the success of this method is simply this: Did the "key" open up a new and deeper understanding of the Scripture passage? If this does not happen, the method has failed, no matter how skilfully it may be used.

Since this method is especially adapted to an auxiliary used with other methods, it can serve as a check and supplement to the other methods. In this case, its value may be found in the way it corrects or illuminates the other method.

Universal Use

When any passage of Scripture is read, the search for the "key" should be in the back of one's mind. Even when other methods may be more effective in presenting the message of the text, the "key" may be the first clue to a proper understanding by the interpreter. No method could have a wider application or offer more possibilities for effective interpretation of the Scriptures.

Epilogue

The coming of a new life into the world is surely one of the most thrilling and awesome experiences within the whole range of human existence. But the dawning of a new idea, the emerging of a new insight, or the opening up of a new vista on the meaning of life can be just as exciting. Life grows stale when it is allowed to stumble along in the old ruts, grinding out the days and weeks in endless monotony. Men are literally perishing for a word "from beyond." They are looking up and hoping for something which will give meaning and purpose to life. They need the life-giving power of a new discovery of themselves and what they can become in the eternal purpose of God.

This is where the biblical interpreter comes in. In all the long history of man's pilgrimage upon this earth, there is only one authentic "Word from beyond." It is the Word made flesh, the living reality of Jesus Christ—God's greatest gift to man. The Bible is the unique book about him. It prepares for his coming, and it records his matchless story.

Because the Bible is the exclusive record and supreme witness of Christ's unique life, it is a unique book. To look into its pages is to see the depth of God's eternal purpose. God "chose us in him before the foundation of the world" (Eph.

1:4). His love is written in the stars. Like a beacon to guide us, this purpose of God points the way through all our confusion and doubt. History is going somewhere—God is guiding it in spite of all of man's sin. Only in the Bible is this message to be found. Men are literally dying to hear this Word from above.

The Romance of the Word

Few thrills can equal the thrill of discovery which comes when a familiar passage of Scripture is opened up with new depth and meaning. But a second thrill is like unto it—the joy of opening up the Scripture for someone else to see. Lives can be transformed, burdens lifted, hope rekindled. The Word of God is absolutely limitless in its power to transform, regenerate, and inspire. No higher calling can be found than the calling to unfold the Word of God to waiting hearts. Every line in this book is intended to quicken this desire to become a channel by which God's Word can come to men today.

Any method of interpretation is useless unless there is the deep desire to understand and share the message of the Scriptures. But anyone who has ever known the joy of seeing the Word come alive in his own heart, or in the hearts of his hearers, will never be the same again. He has been touched by a holy fire, and it will burn in his bones as long as he lives. He can never escape its claim.

It is to serve this purpose that this book was written. It is intended to give inspiration and specific guidance in interpreting the Bible. All the good intentions in the world cannot result in effective interpretation unless there is skill and knowledge in the process. God may use us in spite of our ignorance, but he cannot use our ignorance. We must offer to him the most devoted study and most skilful research of which we are capable. He can use such effort to work the miracle of understanding—to bring the Word alive in our hearts today.

Preparing to Open Up the Scriptures

Nothing is more important to the interpreter than the attitude of expectancy. It is the attitude of faith. When we come to the Scriptures with the sure anticipation of a thrilling word from God, we are thereby opening the door to receive it. The opening moments of any Bible class or any sermon should be spent in creating this attitude of expectancy. Only those who wait upon the Lord will receive his strength.

Every possible channel should be opened up to the flow of the divine Word. Because the interpreter knows the applications of the particular Scripture to contemporary life, he should prepare the way. If it is relevant to family, or work, or nation, then he should spell out the areas of need to which the biblical Word will speak. Let the listener anticipate the meaning of the Word for each life situation, and sometimes he will get there before you do—making the "discovery" for himself. It strikes with even greater force when this is the case. It will etch its way indelibly into his memory.

Seizing the Opportunity

Most people have an image of the biblical interpreter as a preacher in the pulpit, or a Sunday School teacher in the classroom. This is a formal teaching situation and involves great possibilities for encountering the Word of God. However, even more opportunities are offered in the normal contacts of daily life. The casual contact on the job or the family conversation at the table may offer a tremendous opportunity for opening up a new insight on life.

Anyone who studies the Bible faithfully will often be startled by the fact that the very point he has been studying is so applicable to a situation which arises that very day or week. This is because the Word of God is relevant to life—nothing is more relevant. It does speak to our daily needs and applies directly to the problems of life. An alert interpreter of the Bible will seize every opportunity to share the latest insight or discovery from the pages of God's Word.

The best way to prepare for these all-important casual opportunities is to keep up a program of regular Bible study. If the Scriptures are being opened and studied carefully on a regular basis, the opportunities to share them will multiply at an astounding rate. This does not imply the all too common pattern of "arguing the Scriptures" or preaching at people in an offensive way. But it does imply the deep faith that God has a Word for our confused and troubled lives, and that the serious study of his Word as written in the Holy Scriptures will throw light upon our problems and guide us in the right pathway.

Come Alive

The most important single factor in the thrilling experience of interpreting the Bible is the spiritual experience of the interpreter. The study of language, archaeology, and history, important as they are, can never supply the spark which is necessary to bring the message alive for people today. Nothing is more revealing of the inner spiritual life of a person than how he reads and interprets the Bible. His intimate prayer life, his personal relationship to Jesus Christ, and his love for his fellowman will all be revealed in depth as he seeks to unfold the message of the Scriptures.

This book is a plea for people to wake up and live in the joy of Christ. There is no joy like the joy we have in him—forgiveness which goes to the very center of our being; the fellowship of his Holy Spirit in every aspect of life; the unshakable promise of eternal life in Christ, with the glow which this already gives to our new life in him. Before the Word can come alive for others to whom we minister, it must come alive in our own hearts. The Word who became flesh long ago in Bethlehem of Judea must become flesh again in us. Only then can we become instruments through whom the Word may come alive for those whose lives we touch.